College Is Broken

How To Create A Life of Wealth & Freedom
While Most Graduates Are Broke, Stressed,
& Moving Back In With Their Parents

Chelsea Creekmore

Published by Prominence Publishing
www.prominencepublishing.com

ISBN: 978-1-988925-44-8

I gift this book to

_____

because I care about your future success.

Table of Contents

Dedication

To my husband, Cory, for his unwavering support through all the late nights and low points. The path to seven figures has been a wild ride, and there is no one I'd rather have taken it with.

Letter to the Reader: Why College is Broken

Have you ever wanted to burn your diploma? I have, on many occasions, and no—I'm not an arsonist. I'm not against higher education and I'm not ungrateful for the hard work of my professors. I want to torch my degree because of the false promise it represents in our society: the unspoken promise that if you invest 4-8+ years of your life in college and go 5 to 6-figures in debt, your degree will set you on the path to greatness. A path that leads to your dream career, financial freedom, and finding your life's purpose.

Eager students across the globe are following the well-intentioned advice of their parents, teachers, and guidance counselors without understanding the sad truth: college offers no guarantee of success or stability post-graduation. There's a surprisingly high chance you'll graduate with a $24,000 - $78,000[1] piece of paper and struggle to land a good job, or land the job you thought you wanted and find out you hate it. According to a recent Gallup poll, eighty-five percent of workers worldwide admit to hating their jobs when surveyed anonymously.[2] What if the light at the end of the educational tunnel is a job that makes you miserable? On average, a whopping 34% of all college graduates end up at jobs that don't require degrees. As of September 2019, 41.3% of recent college graduates were underemployed. That means 41.3% of graduates spend four or more years working through college to end up at a job they could've landed straight out of high school.[3]

Okay, so 41.3% of people have to make ends meet until they can get their first "real" job. What's the big deal? Making ends meet at a job that doesn't require a degree fresh out of college can be detrimental to your career. Recent graduates who are under-employed earn around $10,000 less than those who are appropri-ately employed in jobs that match their levels of education. Those who are underemployed in their first job are five times more likely to remain underemployed after five years. *Five times.*[4]

As of 2018, 17% of workers in service occupations, like baris-tas and restaurant servers, have a Bachelor's degree or higher.[5] 4+ years of your life and tens of thousands of dollars (or more!) in debt is a lot to trade for a career making unicorn frappucinos. And how many pumpkin spice lattes are you going to have to pour to pay off that debt?

The average cost for all institutions in the 2017-2018 academic year was nearly $24,000, which is 25% higher than the cost of col-lege in the 2007-2008 academic year and 62% higher than the cost of college in the 1997-1998 academic year, adjusted for inflation.[6] Meanwhile, median household income has only increased 5% between 1998 and 2018, adjusted for inflation.[7] Moreover, the co-hort default rate (CDR) on student loans is 10.1%.[8] So basically, if you go to college, there's almost a 1 in 10 chance you'll end up folding clothes or flipping burgers, and a 1 in 10 chance you won't be able to afford your student loan payments. Where's my lighter?

In 2018, 10% of graduates with a bachelor's degree or higher who are between 25 and 37 years old were living with their par-ents. This is higher than previous generations at the same age.[9] According to a recent survey, "half (50%) of young millennials who are currently enrolled or who intend to go to college plan to move back home after."[10] Today's students are graduating un-deremployed and so financially strained they're having to move back in with mom and dad.

Let me be clear: I'm not saying college is bad. If you want to be a doctor or a lawyer, a degree isn't optional. If I were to go back in time, I'd probably still go to college. If it weren't for college, my husband and I wouldn't be married. I wouldn't have found some of my dearest friends. I may have been thrust into a different path that didn't lead me to entrepreneurship if I didn't go to college, and I definitely wouldn't be writing this book. I had professors and programs at the University of Kentucky that really helped shape me. Unfortunately, it wasn't enough. I graduated with a business degree, yet no clue how to actually start a business; in a mountain of debt with no clue how to manage my finances. I had no idea how competitive the job market would be. How had I spent so much of my life in school, yet never been taught how to nail an interview, land a job, get out of debt, build wealth, or launch a company in the entirety of a business degree? But thank god I learned how to balance chemical equations!

College is broken. The entire system needs a complete overhaul, but it's not going to happen overnight. Today's college graduates have two options: Start the slow climb up the corporate ladder (if you're lucky enough to land a job) or refuse to settle for an average lifestyle and average income. If you are reading this book, you are refusing to settle for average. You're hungry to succeed in your career, start a business, write a book, become famous, or achieve whatever magnificent dream moves you. You want to be financially free and, most of all, wildly happy.

In the following chapters, I've laid out everything I wish I was taught in my college classes. I explain how self-education made me a millionaire, and how you can become one too. As Jack Canfield once said, "Everything you want is on the other side of fear." In this book, I'll guide you to the other side. Whether you attended a university, or the school of life, it's time to make your alma mater proud.

PHASE 1

Becoming a BOSS

Chapter 1

Starting the Climb to Seven Figures

College was an invaluable experience for me. Throughout this time, I polished my ability to study and caffeinated myself into meeting deadlines. I learned countless equations, definitions, and theories. I also discovered I could chug a beer in 3.4 seconds. Most importantly, college transformed me from an irresponsible teenager into a semi-functioning adult. It forced me to get out on my own, grow up, and learn to manage my own finances. Turns out, I didn't have to eat ramen noodles or drink Nati Light if I skipped my biweekly trips to the nail salon. This was my level of financial literacy when I graduated college: "I'll have enough money to eat Chipotle and drink craft beer if I skip the nail salon."

Skipping the nail salon was a good move, yes, but galaxies away from the financial literacy of a millionaire. Did I strive to be a millionaire at this time in my life? Absolutely not. Don't get me wrong, I fantasized about flying around in private jets and drinking unreasonably expensive champagne, but that's all it was—a fantasy. The idea of striving to actually earn a million dollars seemed foolish, impossible, and greedy.

Why did a million dollars seem unfathomable to me? Looking back, many factors came into play. Throughout my entire education, we were told to "Learn _____; you'll need to know it next year." "Learn _____; you'll be tested on it in eighth grade." "Learn _____; you have to know it in high school." "Learn _____ if you want to be successful in college." And my favorite, spoken from the mouths of countless college professors: "Employers are looking for candidates who know _____." I knew how to study for next year's curriculum, but after I marched across the stage in my cap and gown, I quickly realized the rest of my life didn't have a curriculum. I went to college because I believed it would set me up for a successful career and a life of wealth, but financial success wasn't even *mentioned* in any of my classes. Student loans taught me to finance things I couldn't afford with debt—a habit which, if kept throughout life, basically guarantees you'll never be wealthy. Education primed me to plug and chug, spit out the right answers, earn my degree, and then ... *hopefully* get a job? My classes didn't even *touch* on how to nail an interview, which is arguably more important than GPA or your major when job hunting. If you graduate cum laude but flop every interview, you'll find it really difficult to land a good job. I was beginning to think this whole "college" thing was a conspiracy.

"Did you find a job yet?" asked *every adult ever* in the months leading up to graduation. Luckily, my answer was yes. I'd taken it upon myself to learn how to nail an interview and accepted a job at an internet training company. My role would be to help car dealerships close more sales from the internet. I could make up to $70,000 per year depending on how many trainings I wanted to take on and how much I wanted to travel. Some of the other trainers were making $80,000 to $90,000 per year. I felt like I'd won the lottery. Adults praised and congratulated me, and it felt good. Society and the education system had so deeply cemented the 9-to-5 in my brain that I didn't even consider other options. It *did not once* cross my mind to start my own business.

Then the unthinkable happened. About two weeks before I graduated, my company "restructured" my position. I would now work as a Client Relations Manager with a base salary of $30,000 with the possibility of making up to $50,000 if I took on enough local training sessions, with no traveling. The problem was, demand for local training sessions was slim to none. I was deflated and angry. I'd make $34,000 a year, at best. I'd turned down multiple job offers in the $40,000 to $45,000 range just a few months prior.

I called my father to vent and ask for his advice. My dad owned a thriving window treatment business, Stamper's Blinds Gallery. He sold custom blinds and shutters, high-end stuff. He was absolutely overwhelmed with business at the time, and I was partly to thank for that. Throughout my internship at the internet training company, I'd learn a marketing strategy that helped a car dealership grow and then apply it to my dad's business. I built him a simple website. I learned the basics of Search Engine Optimization (SEO) to get his website ranking higher on Google. I experimented with Facebook and Google AdWords. This was early 2013, so I definitely wasn't early to the internet marketing world, but my dad's competitors were absolute dinosaurs compared to me. Half of them didn't even have a website. So even though his website was ugly, and I was experimenting, Stamper's hit the million-dollar mark in sales for the first time ever, with a large chunk of their leads coming from the internet.

After hearing about my pay cut, my dad offered two solutions: (1) He would beat up my boss, or (2) If I wanted to follow in his footsteps and start my own business, he would be my first client. Again, I hadn't even considered starting my own business until this time. He would pay me what he previously paid his old internet marketing firm, which would be enough to scrape by. I'd made a huge impact on his business; why not do the same for other small businesses?

My soon-to-be husband was a penny-pincher and we had a wedding to save for, so I wasn't sure how he'd react. However, he *loved* the idea and believed in me wholeheartedly. Fresh out of college and twenty-two years old, we didn't have much to lose. It's not like we had a mortgage to pay or other mouths to feed. If there was ever going to be a time, it was now. On March 31, 2013, I officially launched Creekmore Marketing. I spent the day in pajamas designing a crappy logo, buying a domain name, creating business cards, and blundering my way through my Secretary of State business registration until I had officially launched a Limited Liability Company, or LLC.

Fast forward five years, and Creekmore Marketing is on track to hit over $3 million in sales for 2019. We're a prominent woman-owned business in Kentucky that acts as the outsourced marketing arm for nearly 200 businesses across the United States. I have offices, a team of forty people, and a well-known name in my industry. The road to seven figures wasn't a straight shot. It was filled with twists and turns, tempting shortcuts, and seemingly never-ending hills. But I persisted, just as you will.

If seven figures in the bank is our destination, then most of our society is taking the back roads or driving in the wrong direction. This includes many of your coaches, professors, and parents who have shaped your outlook on success since the day you were born. Yes, they want what's best for you, but they can't give you directions when they haven't been there themselves. They tell you to play it safe and pay your dues, and most college grads follow blindly as they're guided down the road to mediocrity.

But not you.

In the following chapters, I'll give you my seven-figure road map, a turn-by-turn guide to the road less traveled. I'll tell you exactly how I became a twenty-seven-year-old millionaire and how you can become one too. This book is broken up into three sections. Part 1 will teach you everything you should've learned in college: how to be a BOSS, build wealth, perfect your résumé, hack interviews, and level up in your career. Not all graduates are ready to dive headfirst into the world of entrepreneurship. In many cases, getting experience and generating income prior to starting your business can be a much more effective strategy. There's also a chance you could land a job at a fast-growing company and experience more wealth and success than you ever imagined. Part 2 focuses on launching your business so you can break free from the 9-to-5 and create limitless earning potential. I'll teach you how to launch your brand, elevate your network, master sales, become an influencer, and most importantly, scale your business. Finally, part 3 will focus on lifestyle design and finding joy in the journey, because a million dollars is *worthless* if you're miserable or too busy to enjoy it.

Don't read this book cover to cover. Instead, stop after each chapter and ask yourself, "How will I execute this? How can I create a habit around this?" Many of the chapters will end with a series of action steps. My goal isn't just to get you pumped up; it's to get you tangible results: first six, then seven figures in the bank. It's to give you the means to travel the world, the freedom to work where you want, when you want, and to give you the immense pleasure of being your own boss.

This book is about *your* future, and the future is yours to create. Let's begin.

Chapter 2

How to Achieve
Any Goal or Dream

Before we jump into specific strategies for landing a high-paying job and building wealth, I'm going to share an incredibly powerful step-by-step process for achieving any goal or dream, no matter how big or small. All successful people leverage this process in one form or another.

Sell Yourself 100% on Why You Want It →
Make the Decision → Believe It Will Happen →
Adjust Your Actions Accordingly

It seems so simple, but think of a goal or dream you can't seem to achieve; chances are, you're falling short on one or more of these steps. Before I earned my first million, I used this process to bring seven figures into my life. I sold myself 100 percent on why I wanted to earn a million dollars. I wanted to help small businesses across the country grow. I wanted to lead a team of inspiring people. And I wanted to live a life of freedom and luxury—with the flexibility to work when I want, where I want. I wanted to be able to buy a plane ticket and fly to the other side of the world on a whim.

Selling myself 100 percent involved ignoring or changing any thought patterns that were holding me back from joining the million dollar club. I had to argue with my internal naysayer who would frequently ask, "What if?" and then play out worst-case scenarios in my head.

- "What if I end up working my life away?" **I'll find a way to work smarter.**

- "What if I don't have time for my family or friends?" **I'll find a way to make time.**

- "What if my friends and family members get jealous?" **We'll talk it out.**

- "What if I become some self-absorbed, money-hungry prick?" **I won't let myself. Money isn't going to make me a bad person. It's going to enrich my life.**

Next, you must rid yourself of excuses. This process is similar, but instead of "What Ifs," think of all the excuses someone who is pursuing this dream might make and counter them.

- "I have no clue where to start." **I'll find someone who has done it before and learn from them, either in person or on social media.**

- "I don't have time." **I'll make time. Everyone has the same twenty-four hours in a day. It's about priorities, not time.**

- "I don't have the experience." **I'll get the experience. I'll take an online training course, watch videos, get a job in the field, shadow someone, or practice on my own.**

- "I don't have the money." **I'll figure out how to earn the money.** *(More on this in chapters 8, 9, and 10)*

- "There's too much competition." **I'll find a way to be different. Yes, people have done it before, but *no one* will do it like I will.**

If you're 100 percent sold, arguing with your internal naysayer is a cakewalk. Do it consistently enough and you can shut him or her down for good.

Be sure to do your research during this phase and take *very few* opinions. Talk to successful people in your industry who have achieved what you want to achieve and take advice from them. While it's nice to talk to friends, family, or people who are just starting out, chances are they can't inspire you or guide you quite like someone who has been there. If they are struggling themselves, they may steer you in the wrong direction or demotivate you.

Once I 100 percent sold myself on why I wanted to become a millionaire, I made the decision to pursue it. I wrote it down on the top of my goals list and made a vision board. I wrote down everything I would do with the money once I earned it. I committed to pursuing this dream no matter what.

From here, I convinced myself it would happen. A big part of this was continuing to argue with my internal nay-sayer, the voice of fear, each time she reared her ugly head. Every time I had a negative thought, I would flip it into a positive and empowering one. I walked through the richest neighborhoods in town and imagined myself living in one of those mansions with a paid-off mortgage, telling myself over and over that I would make it happen. Lastly, I controlled what I fed my mind. If it wasn't motivational audiobooks, podcasts, or YouTube videos that fell in line with my vision, I wasn't watching it or listening to it. Your mind is constantly absorbing the information you feed it, and it's *so* important to control that message. Negative media will only distract and discourage you from pursuing your dreams. Listening to positive messages from people who inspire you can completely change your mental state and outlook on life. If you feed your mind enough motivation and positivity, you'll find it difficult *not* to believe your dreams will come true.

Lastly, I adjusted my actions accordingly. I worked fourteen-hour days, took countless training courses, researched my industry, and figured out what customers hated most about internet marketing firms so I could position myself differently. I made countless mistakes and learned from them. I went above and beyond to connect with and provide value to every person I met. I delivered amazing customer service, even if it meant calling my clients in Hawaii during my dinner time or solving client issues on the weekends. (Don't worry—I didn't have to do this forever. I consider my first few years in business my grind phase and have set much healthier work/life boundaries now.) There were so many times where I felt like giving up, but being 100 percent sold on the vision gave me the determination to push through. I didn't have one big break. I had to earn every penny of that seven figures by selling and then going above and beyond to deliver on the promises I made.

The Key to Action Is Developing Habits

Unless your goal is to lose half a pound or write one page of a book, your actions need to be consistent over time. This can be challenging when you dream big. Maybe you have no clue where to start, or the mere thought of working toward your goal feels exhausting. Any long-term goal can be attained by breaking it into smaller parts and developing a daily habit to help you achieve it. When I decided to write this book, I committed to writing 500 words per day. I determined that if I wanted to write a 50,000-word book, each day that I wrote 500 words, I was completing 1 percent of my book. I used a daily planner to mark what percentage of completion I'd reached. I started out with about 15 percent in March 2018 from thoughts I'd collected over the previous few years. By April 1, I'd reached 42 percent. By May 1, 67 percent. And by June 1, I'd finished my first draft.

So how do you make a new habit? It's both simpler and more complicated than you might think. You might have heard the old adage that if you do the same thing once a day for twenty-one days or thirty days, it will become a habit, but this actually is not the case.[11] A research team based out of University College London performed a study on ninety-six university students who agreed to try out a new healthy habit once a day for twelve weeks to see when they reported generally feeling like the behavior was automatic, or habitual.

The median amount of time it took participants to form a new habit was sixty-six days, way longer than the twenty-one or thirty days you might have been told.[12] But ultimately, the results varied from person to person and from goal to goal. Typically, simpler goals had a quicker uptake than more complicated goals, so someone wanting to drink a bottle of water every day is probably going to have an easier time than someone who wants to do a whole yoga flow before breakfast in the morning.

Take this book, for example; it's important to note that in the beginning, writing 500 words seemed impossible. I had to force myself to get in the zone and get motivated to write. Sometimes clicking the keys felt like dragging nails down a chalkboard. About a month in, I realized the words were flowing effortlessly for me each day. I'd figured out how to get in the right mind-set, I was building momentum, and I had blocked time in my calendar every morning to write. I had designed my life and trained my brain to make something easy that once felt impossible. If you want to learn how to develop positive habits to achieve your goal by making small changes in your life, I highly recommend *The Power of Habit* by Charles Duhigg and *The Compound Effect* by Darren Hardy.

Develop Morning Routines that Fuel Your Habits

If you want to be successful, your number-one goal every morning should be to get yourself inspired. It's just as important as brushing your teeth. When I wanted to finish writing my book, I woke up every morning, took a walk, and listened to the podcast *Please, Finish Your Book!* by Shola Richards. I then switched to *The War of Art: Break through the Blocks and Win Your Inner Creative Battles* by Steven Pressfield. Feed your mind motivation that is *relevant* to your goals and what you're struggling with in the moment—not just motivation for motivation's sake.

"But Wait—I'm a Skeptic!"

If you're still struggling to make yourself believe, fake it until you make it. You may not feel confident at first, and that's okay. The only thing that builds confidence is taking action. If you make mistakes, great. Now you know what *not* to do. When you succeed, you'll build confidence, which will make future actions and habits easier.

You can use this four-step process to achieve anything, from the smallest of goals to the wildest of dreams. Maybe you want to lose ten pounds, eat healthier, get a promotion, write a book, or start a side business. In the following chapters, I'll help you develop the mind-set and skill-set to make any dream a reality.

My wildest dream was to become an author, and here you are, reading these words right now. I can tell you from experience that anything is possible if you sell yourself on why you want it, make the decision, believe, and adjust your actions accordingly. There are people less qualified than you doing the things you want to do, simply because they followed this process and chose to believe in themselves.

Boss's Action Plan:

1. What's that thing you can't stop thinking about? Maybe it's a career, goal, or idea. One that makes your heart leap, but also seems so far-fetched you feel stupid for even thinking it or embarrassed to tell your friends and family about it? That's your wildest dream.

2. Write it down. Say it out loud. Admit it to yourself and feel that rush of adrenaline and excitement flood your body.

3. To sell yourself 100 percent on why you want it, write down all of your "What Ifs." Pretend a skeptic is asking these questions. Now, argue back with that person.

4. Next, write down every excuse you can think of *not* to pursue your dream, and argue back.

5. Make the decision and commit to pursuing your dream relentlessly.

6. Convince yourself it will happen by surrounding yourself with positivity and inspiration. Listen to motivational audiobooks, podcasts, or YouTube videos that are relevant to your vision. Catch yourself when you're being negative and flip the switch.

7. Set aside time in your schedule to take action *this week* and every week until you've reached your goal.

8. Tell a close friend or family member about your wildest dream. If they support you, great! If they tell you you're crazy, let the doubt fuel you—you're going to remember that when you make it big.

Chapter 3

Three Types of People

Achievers go the extra mile.
Bosses go the extra marathon.
Settlers don't even register for the race.

There are three types of people in this world: settlers, achievers, and bosses. A majority of the population falls into the first two categories, settlers or achievers. In fact, our society and education system primes us to think these are our only two options. We praise achievers, who play by the rules, get good grades, a good degree, and a good job so they can start the slow climb up the seemingly never-ending corporate ladder. We then kick settlers in the tail, telling them to get their acts together and be more like the achievers.

But there are people succeeding at a higher level: bosses. No, I'm not referring to boss in the managerial sense. Think of it more as a synonym for badass. These are the artists, authors, creatives, businesspeople, and individuals who *refuse* to be average, so they either break the rules or create their own game. Bosses don't buy into societal pressures or norms. They don't believe in paying their dues and brownnosing for thirty years hoping it'll take their career to a new level. These are debt-free homeowners, young entrepreneurs, and self-made millionaires. They firmly believe in the saying, "If opportunity doesn't knock, build a door."

We've all been settlers, achievers, and bosses at different times in our lives. In some areas, we absolutely have our act together, and in other areas, we fall short, but if you really want to earn seven figures, consistency is key. You must learn to think and act like a boss day in and day out. I'm not going to lie to you; it's tough. It took me years to level up to the place I'm at now, and I'm still working on myself every day. I still make mistakes *every day*. Self-improvement is a journey that never ends.

I'm going to share commonly held beliefs of all three groups so you can determine where you fall. The point of this is not to make you feel bad, but to show you the mentality you must develop to level up. Be brutally honest with yourself as you read these beliefs. If you sound like a settler, don't get discouraged. Get excited because you have huge opportunities to grow and improve your life. And if you sound like an achiever, you should be proud. Being an achiever is a good thing. You're one step away from that next level—the level that has the power to give you anything and everything you want in life.

BELIEFS	SETTLERS	ACHIEVERS	BOSSES
Worldview	Hold rigid negative attitudes about the world.	Hold positive and negative attitudes about the world.	Believe in their ability to change their world. Actively focus on the positive and ways they can either improve or disengage with the negative.
Skepticism	Assume most people are selfish, disingenuous, and have ulterior motives.	Strive to see the good in *most* people.	Bring out the good in everyone around them by always giving others the benefit of the doubt.
Debt	Believe debt is a part of life.	Try to minimize debt.	Fiercely eliminate debt.
Money Mind-set	Believe money is the root of all evil and that rich people are greedy.	Believe money is important, but don't want to hustle too hard and seem money hungry.	Have no shame about desiring wealth. Money makes dreams come true and allows you to live life to the fullest.
Availability of Money	Believe there isn't enough money to	Believe they have earning potential,	Believe their income potential is

BELIEFS	SETTLERS	ACHIEVERS	BOSSES
	go around. Often find themselves riddled with jealousy when someone else gets rich.	within "reason." Have difficulty believing they can earn money in a way that isn't tied to their time.	limitless. Understand that if someone else gets rich, it doesn't lessen their chances of becoming a millionaire.
Money Excuses	"Life isn't all about money. I'm not going to sacrifice the more important things in life to get rich."	"If you work hard, you will have enough."	"Money will give me the freedom to live life abundantly. Getting rich will give me more time and means to focus on the important things in life."
Financial Savvy	Spend without saving or investing. Will *never* be rich no matter how much money they make.	Spend within reason. Save and dabble with investments. May be comfortable in life, but not necessarily rich.	Live like a poor college kid until they've eliminated debt, then move on to investing. Commit to improving their financial knowledge and aren't afraid to bring in an expert for guidance. Will find a way to become rich no matter what.
Asking	"Don't bother asking. It's no use."	"Ask and you shall receive."	"Provide enough value and you'll be amazed at how often you receive without even having to ask. But if you don't receive, ask until you do."
Toughness	Not very tough because they care to a fault. Constantly worry about what others think of them.	Care what other people think of them, within reason.	Take *very* few opinions. Work on themselves daily to develop an unshakable sense of self-worth and confidence to the point that it doesn't matter

BELIEFS	SETTLERS	ACHIEVERS	BOSSES
			what other people think of them.
Excuses	"I was late because of the traffic."	"Sorry I'm late."	"I should've left earlier. It won't happen again." And it doesn't.
Success	"Success is for snobs and ass-kissers."	"Success is mine to take."	"The more I help others succeed, the more I succeed."
Recognition	Take credit when it's not theirs to take.	Take credit as often as possible, when they've earned it.	Strive to give others credit whenever possible.
Work	Live for the weekends and vacations. Wake up every day dreading their jobs.	Very responsible and hardworking, but rarely takes risks.	Cultivate feelings of gratitude toward their work, no matter what it is.
Work Ethic	Do the bare minimum to get paid.	Work hard for decades, from graduation until retirement.	Work harder and smarter while they're young so they can experience a life most people would only dream of.

Where did you fall? Most people are scattered across the board in multiple categories. And remember, most of our society isn't even aware of the boss category. But of course, most of our society will never become millionaires.

If you're mostly a settler, you're going to have one hell of a comeback story to tell. And if you're mostly an achiever, I can't wait to show you what that next level will do for your happiness and your bank account.

Chapter 4

The CVI Assessment

The Ultimate Life Hack: Knowing Yourself

My mentor Peter Voogd—author of the best-selling book *6 Months to 6 Figures*—introduced me to a concept that changed my life. In a training I attended through his Gamechanger's Academy, he said: "What you don't know about yourself controls your entire life. And what you don't understand about others, controls your business."

He encouraged me to take a *Core Values Index* assessment (CVI), which is similar to a personality test. I was skeptical. How could who I am as a person be accurately assessed in ten minutes? I expected gimmicky, catchall responses of personality traits that could arguably apply to anyone.

How wrong I was. The results were mind-blowing. It's like someone cracked open my skull, studied the gears turning, and unpacked my personal operating manual. I uncovered secrets I was never consciously aware of about who I am, my strengths, and my weaknesses.

This is important because knowing yourself and leveraging your strengths is crucial if you want to earn seven figures. If your job role conflicts with your core values, chances are, you will find it *impossible* to be satisfied in your career and extremely difficult to land raises, promotions, or new clients. A job that conflicts with your core values forces you to focus on your areas of weakness. If you really want to level up, you need a career that plays to your strengths. Most seven-figure earners spend very little time trying to improve upon their weaknesses. They focus on leveraging their strengths and automating, outsourcing, or delegating their weaknesses. It's better to be the *best* at one thing than mediocre at everything.

The thing is, we don't always know where our true strengths and weaknesses lie. So many people choose majors based on what feels interesting at the time, what their parents want, or what society tells them is a "good field." Fast forward five to ten years, and they're in a job they can't stand, doing work that makes them miserable. They're frustrated that they can't take their career or business to the next level and can't seem to figure out why.

Had they taken a CVI assessment in college, it could've saved them *years* of frustration and stagnation in their career. I highly recommend you take it yourself before moving on to the next chapter. The assessment takes ten minutes or less and can be found here: https://members.taylorprotocols.com/Tools/CVIGift.aspx?GiftHash=262a9bc0-bd2e-1035-9042-91cd512dec1c. (I am not affiliated with CVI or Taylor Protocols. I simply love what they're doing!)

There are four core values: Builder (Power), Merchant (Love), Innovator (Wisdom), and Banker (Knowledge). Builders value results and action, Merchants value vision and relationships, Innovators value assessment and solutions, and Bankers value conservation and information. I scored as a Merchant-Innovator, with Builder as a close third. Your two core values should come naturally, and your third value could likely use development. Oftentimes, mastering your third value is what will take your life and business to the next level.

The CVI taught me how to stop spinning my wheels in my business. It helped me figure out exactly what I should be spending my time on to be most effective and happy. It taught me what type of people I should surround myself with to complement my weaknesses. On a personal level, it drastically improved my relationships with my husband, friends, and coworkers. Understanding what drives someone allows you to speak in their language, which can be the difference between someone liking you or disliking you, trusting you or wanting to keep you at arm's length, writing you off or buying into *every word* you have to say. This information is invaluable if you want to enjoy your career, connect with your manager, coworkers, or clients, and deepen your relationships with friends and family.

In the next few chapters, I'll show you how bosses craft résumés, hack interviews, and level up in the corporate world. These skills can legitimately be the difference between flipping burgers after college or landing a salaried job at a fast-growing company.

"But I'm Ready to Start My Own Business!"

Awesome. You're ahead of the game. Skip the next three chapters. For anyone who isn't quite ready to dive into the entrepreneurial world headfirst, the next three chapters are for you. I'll help you land a job at a company in your desired field, so you can gain experience and steady income before you venture out on your own. Remember, you can always start a side hustle while working full time. And don't completely rule out the corporate world—if you land a job at a fast-growing company and play your cards right, you could achieve the income you desire without the grunt work and risk of starting your own company.

Chapter 5

Résumé on Steroids

A settler's or achiever's résumé isn't going to cut it in today's competitive workforce. A boss's résumé is more than just a professional summary; it's a sales pitch. If it doesn't generate interviews, something is seriously wrong, and in this chapter, I'll show you exactly how to fix it.

As we go through this section, keep in mind that you are the author of your résumé. It's your job to make your work history and strengths pop off the page and make you shine. Even if your work experience is slim or irrelevant to your desired career path, you can portray it in a way that shows your grit and leadership abilities. And be aware that people don't read résumés; they skim. Opt for more bullet points and fewer paragraphs whenever possible. Keep your verbiage simple. There is no need to throw out industry specific jargon or lengthy descriptions that the hiring manager likely won't understand. Instead, identify buzzwords to include by carefully analyzing the job posting. For example, in a management position, you may use words like *leading*, *delegating*, *coordinating*, and *communicating*. You want that person skimming your résumé to think, "Wow. This person is exactly who we're looking for!"

Cover Letters

Maybe the job you're applying for requires a cover letter, maybe it doesn't. Regardless, you should include one because you're taking every opportunity you can to wow the hiring manager. Your cover letter may be an actual letter, or it might be an introductory email or message in an online application portal.

Most application emails I receive are either very generic or blank. Some have clearly been copied and pasted. I can't help but mentally discount those people for putting in little to no effort. What if they put the same effort into the emails they send clients?

The key to wowing with the cover letter is to make it personal and to make the hiring manager feel special, because they are. They hold the key to your future career. Here is an example of a cover letter:

Dear Mrs. Creekmore, (Always include a name, even if you have to scour the internet or call the company.)

Your Marketing Strategist position caught my attention and I'm writing to apply. I would be honored and inspired to work for a company led by a powerful female CEO. (Include something personal and flattering here, something that proves you didn't just copy and paste. Maybe it's about a project the hiring manager has worked on, the type of clients they work with, their leader, or a charity they are involved with. The more specific and genuine, the better.)

I'd be an excellent fit for this position because of my experience and intrinsic motivation to succeed. Throughout my college internships, I've gained extensive experience in social media marketing and search engine optimization. See my attached résumé for details of my accomplishments at each company, which fall in line with this position.

I'd love the opportunity to interview if you feel I'd be a good fit for this position, or any other position at your company.

Thank you,

Signature
Contact Details

Customize Your Résumé and Cover Letter to Match the Job Description

Don't copy and paste verbatim, but definitely include the key phrases from the job description in your résumé and cover letter. When hiring, I had a very detailed job description and ideal candidate description on our website. Maybe one or two of a hundred candidates would write something in their cover letter or application email that clearly proved they had read the job description. No matter the position they were applying for, those applications always stood out from the rest.

It's All in the Delivery

Did you flip burgers or coordinate with servers to ensure food was delivered hot and steaming? Did you have to give some jerk a free meal because he screamed about the fries being cold? Or did you resolve disputes that turned angry patrons into loyal customers? Frame every job experience in a positive light, no matter how menial the responsibilities. Preferably, you'll have more relevant experience than a fast-food job, and if not, you may want to consider arranging a paid or unpaid internship in your field. At Creekmore Marketing, we've been contacted by multiple college graduates looking for internships because they goofed around in school and can't seem to get a job due to lack of relevant experience. If you were a settler in college and are just now realizing that you need to take initiative if you want to level up, don't be afraid to put in the extra effort to find a relevant internship. Even if it's unpaid, that experience will help you get on par with your colleagues, and set you up to exceed them in the future.

And as all good authors know, it's important to show, not tell. Instead of using words like "hardworking" or "excellent communicator," share specific on-the-job achievements that prove you're a hard worker and an excellent communicator. Don't forget to list your responsibilities *and* achievements. Here is an example of what well-organized job experience looks like:

Job Title   Date
ABC Company

- Responsibility #1
- Responsibility #2
- Responsibility #3
- Responsibility #4

Achievements

- Achievement #1
- Achievement #2
- Achievement #3

Lastly, if you're in a creative field or applying at a progressive company, don't be afraid to get creative with your résumé. For years, we were told to keep our résumés black and white, 12-point Times New Roman font. Some of the best résumés I've seen had professional headshots, graphics, charts, and colors. It's a great way to showcase your creativity and design skills, or simply show you put in the extra effort. That being said, know your audience and don't go overboard. Applying with a bright pink résumé to an accounting firm would likely result in a laugh and a toss in the trash can.

Résumé Don'ts

The following are a list of things you should avoid when creating your résumé:

- Listing your high school experience, unless it's impressive.

- Listing obvious skills. We all know how to use Microsoft Word and the internet.

- Squeezing everything onto one page in size 7 font. Go back and take the least important information out.

- Forgetting spellcheck. Triple check your résumé and have a friend proofread it as well.

- Making it generic. Specifically tailor your résumé to each job you apply for.

- Being too general. The following examples could describe the same job, but example B gives the details hiring managers are looking for:

  A. Led a team of sales associates

  B. Hired, trained, and supervised a team of 15 sales associates in a retail setting with over $3 million in annual revenue

Follow-Up Is Key

Wait at least three days, maybe a week, and then follow up about your application with an email or phone call. The goal is to reiterate your interest in the position politely, without putting pressure on the hiring manager. You can say something like, "I'd love to discuss the position further when your schedule allows."

Still Not Getting Interviews?

- **Ask a professional to review your résumé.** Preferably, it would be someone you know who works in a hiring department. Do you need to reword certain things? Remove a section? Is your experience going to stand out, or should you consider applying for an internship or shadowing someone in the field for a couple of months to beef it up? Make any necessary changes and reapply.

- **Send a handwritten card in the mail thanking the hiring manager for the opportunity.** Again, reiterate your interest and how you'd love to discuss the position when he or she is ready to schedule interviews. Worried about bugging the person? The chance of standing out among the other applicants is worth the risk of being a bother. You weren't hearing back anyway, and chances are, you'll never see this person if you don't get the interview. You've got nothing to lose!

- **Add the hiring manager on LinkedIn and send him or her a message.** Make sure you've spaced this out a couple of days between your last contact attempt.

- **Create a video résumé.** This should be a sixty-second or less video of you explaining why you're the ideal candidate for the job. Creating a video résumé helped me land a fantastic internship in college and gain experience that has fueled the rest of my career. It doesn't have to be anything fancy, and yes, you can film it with your phone. Opt for a solid background in an area with lots of natural light. Re-film your video multiple times until you sound natural, genuine, and enthused. And be sure to end your video strong; my ending line was, "I'm intrinsically motivated to succeed. I will come in early, stay late, and go above and beyond to exceed your expectations." I used iMovie to insert my phone number and email address at the bottom of the video. Upload your video privately to YouTube and email it to the hiring manager. If you don't hear back in a few days, send a follow-up message on LinkedIn with the link.

- If you want to use this video for multiple companies, you can. I'd recommend filming a short, custom introduction for each company and leaving the end more general, focusing on you and your work ethic.

Start a conversation with the staff.

- **Contact the blogger who wrote their most recent blog post and compliment it.** As you continue the conversation, mention you've recently applied and hope to get an interview. You never know; the blogger could be close with the hiring manager.

- **Comment on the company's social media posts**. The person who represents the company on social media may have a direct in with the hiring manager or owners of the company.

Drop your résumé and cover letter off in person.

- Some hiring managers will be impressed with your bold-ness and persistence, some will be annoyed. I'll walk you through how to handle both scenarios. I would do this as a last resort if you haven't heard back three or four weeks after applying. At that point, what do you have to lose?

- Go to the store and buy a professional résumé cover or folder for your résumé and cover letter. When you enter the building, tell the first person you see that you recently applied and were hoping to quickly introduce yourself to whoever is in charge of hiring. Ideally, you would ask for this person by name. If you meet him or her, keep it short and sweet. "Hi, I'm so-and-so. I just wanted to drop by and give you my résumé and cover letter. Are you still hiring for X position?" Gauge their interest at this point. If they seem bothered, you can end with, "I'm sure you're busy, so I'll let you get back to it. Sorry to barge in unex-pectedly; I'm just excited about this opportunity. Have a nice day!" If they seem open to the approach, you could ask about the position and the company. You may even get a tour of the place!

As you perfect your résumé and continue to apply, keep your end goal in mind. It could be to get in on the ground floor of a rapidly growing company. It could be to build your résumé and make a steady living while you go after your dreams, whether that be a side business, writing a book, or whatever you are pas-sionate about. Don't just aimlessly wander into the corporate world without a plan or you risk getting stuck in a dead-end job.

Bosses get multiple interview callbacks because they put in ten times the effort achievers do, one hundred times the effort settlers do. They never complain that they "can't get a job," because if opportunity doesn't knock, they'll build a door. Bosses are resilient in their job search and don't take rejection personally. You didn't hear back from a company you really wanted to work at? Follow up. Film a video. Send a card. Do something else to get their attention. They still don't want to hire you? It wasn't meant to be. On to the next one.

Boss's Action Plan:

1. Rework your résumé to highlight your specific accomplishments and leadership abilities that directly correlate with the job description.

2. Less is more. Opt for bullet points and trim it down to fit on one page in a normal, 12-point font. Leave out anything that is obvious or unimpressive.

3. Design your résumé in a way that speaks to your industry and the company you are applying for. If the company is creative, get creative. If the company is traditional, keep it traditional.

4. Get third-party opinions and help proofreading. If you can, get feedback from someone in your field or in a hiring position.

5. Craft a cover letter that is personalized, flattering, and genuine. It should convince the hiring manager you are the perfect person for the job, as well as give the impression this is the only job you are applying for, even if that's not true.

6. Submit your application with your cover letter. Your cover letter may be a separate attachment, an introductory

email, and/or a message on the company's application portal.

7. Wait a few days, maybe a week, then follow up with a phone call or email.

8. If you're still not getting interviews, kick your follow-up into overdrive. Send a handwritten letter, create a video résumé, add key contacts on LinkedIn, etc.

9. Stay positive and keep applying. Just because thirty companies didn't call you back, doesn't mean the thirty-first won't.

In the next chapter, we'll cover everything you need to know about hacking interviews so you have multiple job offers to choose from.

Chapter 6

Hacking Interviews

Were you taught how to nail an interview in college? I wasn't and it still baffles me to this day. I know people who graduated college cum laude and ended up working a drive-thru line. These are high-achieving students who fell flat during their interviews because they didn't know how to sell themselves or wow the hiring manager.

In this chapter, I'll save you the hours and hours of online research I performed to hone my interviewing skills. I had five job offers when I graduated college. During my fifth interview, I told the hiring manager, "Just to give you a head's up, I have four other offers, two of which need an answer by the end of this week." What an interesting role-reversal that was. She scrambled to get me an offer as quickly as possible, and if she had a range of salaries she could offer, I imagine she leaned higher.

This is the position you want to be in. You want to have the hiring managers fighting over *you*. In the following steps, I'll show you exactly how to make that happen.

Step 1: Scheduling the Interview

Your résumé did its job and you're moving on to the interview stage. Nice! Be prepared for the email or phone call to schedule the interview, as it's important to show enthusiasm and gather key information here. "Hey Joe, this is so-and-so hiring manager at XYZ, Inc. We'd like to schedule an interview with you. What's your availability in the next week?"

Joe's response should be, "That's great news! Thank you. Give me one moment to pull up my calendar." (Show enthusiasm here, but don't go overboard. You didn't get the job—yet.)

"I'm available on these dates/times. What works best for you?" And once you nail down a time, ask the following:

- "Who will be conducting the interview?" Get the name(s) if possible, so you can do your homework.

Optional questions if the interview is in-person:

- "What attire would be most appropriate for the interview?" Personally, I never asked this question and always defaulted to business professional, but if you sense the company you are applying for has a particularly casual or unique culture, it can't hurt to ask and shows you're thinking ahead.

- "What is your coffee or tea preference?" I had a candidate ask me this question when I told her we'd meet at a local coffee shop for the interview. I arrived ten minutes early and she was already sitting down with a steaming cup of green tea and a blueberry scone for me. You may roll your eyes and call this "brownnosing," but for me, it showed she was bold, courteous, and willing to go above and beyond. If this isn't your style, feel free to skip this question.

Step 2: Doing Your Homework

- Dig through the company's website and social media profiles. Get a feel for the company's culture. Is it casual or traditional? Rapidly changing or steady?

- Look up and connect with the person(s) interviewing you on LinkedIn, so you can learn more about their background and put a face to a name. This shows initiative and will make you feel more comfortable during the interview, since the person won't be a total stranger. It also helps to understand what generation your interviewer is in, as you will relate to a millennial much differently than you would a baby boomer.

Everyone can google and prepare answers to interview questions that sound professional. However, answers oftentimes mean less than delivery. Do you sound genuine? Excited about the position? Confident? It's okay to sound a bit nervous. Write down your answers to the most common interview questions and practice, practice, practice your answers. My interviews for post-college jobs were very successful because I practiced for hours, like an actress memorizing a script. Then, once my answers were second-nature to me, I practiced for at least another half hour, focusing solely on the delivery of my answers, making sure they came off as genuine, conversational, enthusiastic, and confident. Some people disagree with this advice because over-practicing can make your answers sound robotic—but those people aren't taking the time to practice the delivery once they've got the content down pat.

The hidden questions every interviewer wants to know are:

- Have you done your research? Do you know what we're all about?

- Do you have relevant experience? (Don't worry. You can make any experience relevant.)

- Do you have the skills necessary for this role? And can you handle the challenges in this role?

- Are you a hard worker?

- Are you reliable?

- Do you really want this job? Would you be satisfied in this role?

- Are you going to be here long-term?

- Will you fit in with the company culture?

- Why are you leaving your current job? (If applicable)

It is your responsibility to communicate this information regardless of what questions you're asked.

There are tons of great YouTube videos on how to answer particular interview questions. But for now, I'm going to touch on some popular questions and share exactly how bosses answer to get the job.

"Tell me about yourself."

What they really mean: Tell me about your professional achievements and why you'll be a good fit for this position.

What NOT to Do:

- Ask, "Well, what do you want to know?"

- Tell your life story

- Talk about your kid, partner, dog, or cat (No matter how fluffy and precious they are.)

- Leave out your professional strengths and work history

- Undersell yourself

What they want to hear: You have at least semi-relevant experience. You have the skills needed to excel in this role, as proved through achievements in previous roles. You're confident in your abilities and sold on why you would be an asset to their company. (If you're not sold, how do you expect to sell them on why they should hire you?)

A boss's answer: "I'm an accountant to the core. I just received a BA in accounting with a 3.6 GPA. Throughout my classes and internships, I've sharpened my auditing and financial skills. At ABC company, I worked with smaller firms auditing financial statements, forecasting financial projections, and creating budgets. I know your firm works with larger clientele and that really interests me. I was excited to see this job posting because this position sounds like it was made for me and I know I can be an asset to your firm."

"What is your biggest weakness?"

What they really mean: Can you honestly self-assess and self-improve?

What NOT to Do:

- Mention a weakness that is a fatal flaw for the job. I was replacing a very unorganized account manager who was constantly missing deadlines. Someone I was interviewing said their biggest weakness was, "I have trouble checking things off my to do list, but I'm working on it." I cut the interview short after that, because this was the exact person I was trying to avoid and she didn't really sell me on her ability to overcome this issue.

- Pick a generic weakness that is "secretly" a strength, such as, "I'm a perfectionist." For a while, this was the go-to weakness-but-not-really that many people felt compelled to give as their answer. But, like any good cliché, it has started to sound more and more disingenuous over time. Try to be honest about your weaknesses, but pick a redeemable flaw that you can work to ameliorate, not an Achilles heel.

What they want to hear: You know how to assess yourself and point out your own problems. More importantly, you know how to work through those problems to improve your performance. The key to slaying this question is being genuine.

A boss's answer: "When a new project pops up that excites me, I tend to want to tackle it immediately. But in the past, when I've had other deadlines and projects on my plate, this wasn't always feasible. I've learned I can't just drop everything and tackle what I'm enthusiastic about. Through reading books about time management and exercising willpower, I've really improved at prioritizing and blocking chunks of focus time to knock out important projects and make sure I hit every deadline every time."

"What is your biggest strength?"

What NOT to Do:

- List strengths and hope they take your word for it

- Say things that could be misconstrued as weaknesses. Maybe you work long hours and late nights because you struggle with time management.

What they want to hear: You can give proof of your strengths by highlighting specific examples.

A boss's answer: "My biggest strength is my work ethic. At my previous job, our website went down while my manager was on vacation. It was 6:00 p.m. and the web developer wasn't answering my phone calls. So I stayed late, and even though I have no experience with web design, I googled and watched YouTube videos on DNS settings and a bunch of other things that were Greek to me until I was able to restore the website. I will do whatever it takes to help myself, my team, and my company succeed."

"Where do you see yourself in five years?"

What they really mean: Is this job a good fit for you? Will you be here long term?

What NOT to do:

- Talk about your dream job in a completely different field

- Mention your aspirations to move across the country

- Say anything that would conflict with you being the ideal candidate for this job

- Be phony

What they want to hear: This job is the perfect fit for me. I will be happy in this role for as long as you need me in it, but I would love to take on more responsibility and move into a leadership role if given the opportunity.

A boss's answer: "I'd like to be making a difference at a company like yours. My goal is to become an expert in my role so that everyone I interact with is grateful I'm a part of the team. For most people, five years of experience is one year of experience repeated five times over. For me, my personal mission will be to grow each year so that I may contribute as much as I possibly can to my team, upper management, and our clients, whether

I'm still in this role or have been given the opportunity to move into a leadership position."

"What do you know about us?"

What they really mean: How much did you actually research us?

What they want to hear: Yes, I researched everything I could find about your company, and I'd fit in perfectly with your culture.

A boss's answer: "I know you primarily offer website and graphic design for CPA firms. You recently won a prestigious award for your graphic design work with Ackley Associates. I saw the work on Facebook; it was phenomenal. When I read your mission statement, that's when I knew I had to do whatever it takes to get this interview. I loved the part that said, 'We bring your brand to life and get just as excited to unveil it to the world as you do.' That really spoke to me because I invest 100 percent in everything I do and I get excited about the end result, no matter how big or small the project is. But of course, I just know what I've read online. Could you tell me more about the company from your experience?"

"Why did you leave your last job?"

What they mean: Are you going to leave us for the same reasons?

What they want to hear: My reason to leave there is going to be one of my reasons to stay here.

A boss's answer: "My previous job wasn't salaried or necessarily very stable. I'm looking for a more stable, long-term career which is why this job piqued my interest."

Why were you fired?

What they want to hear: The truth and how you've learned from the experience.

Now, you may be tempted to play the blame game, but paradoxically, the more personal responsibility you show for the situation, the better.

A boss's answer: "I was fired because I was in charge of a project that tanked. It was a six-month-long graphic design project that resulted in the client getting very upset and wanting a full refund. Some of my team members said this was the type of customer who would never be happy no matter what you do, but to me, that's not a good enough excuse. Looking back, I wish I'd taken the time to meet with him in person more often and build that connection. I wish I had called more frequently to smooth things over when he didn't like the direction we were going. I hate the way things ended with XYZ company, but I learned a very valuable lesson that I'll carry with me the rest of my career and I feel more prepared to handle a project like this than I ever did before. And if there is any shred of doubt in your mind that I'm the perfect candidate for this position, I'd be so grateful for a chance to prove to you that I am."

Why do you want this job?

What they want to hear: I would be happy at this job and I would be an asset to your team.

A boss's answer: "I want this job because this is exactly where I envisioned my career going. I would be really happy in this role. And with my skills and experience, I truly feel I'd be an asset to your team."

Why should we hire you over the other candidates who have applied?

What they want to hear: That you can confidently sell them on why you're the perfect candidate without bashing the other candidates.

A boss's answer: "I can't speak to the other candidates, but you should hire me because I'm intrinsically motivated to succeed and I never make excuses. I'll meet with that angry customer to smooth things out. I'll take on that tedious project everyone else is dreading. I will come early, stay late, and do whatever it takes to exceed your expectations, while helping my team members in any way I possibly can."

During your interview process, you may be asked an unexpected question and be forced to think on your feet. Go ahead and plan for it now. The easiest way to do this is to come up with a few real-life examples you can share, and explain them by starting with the situation, the action you took to resolve or improve the situation, and the end result. I recommend the following:

- A time you exercised leadership

- A conflict you've faced at work and how you handled it

- A time you disagreed with a decision made at work

- An example of how you handled a stressful situation

- An explanation of how your coworkers or manager would describe you

I've also heard of people asking, "What's the weirdest thing we would find in your fridge?" This question is to test how you think on your feet, how creative you are, and perhaps if you would fit into the company's quirky culture. I've also heard of questions like, "How many baseballs could you fit in a limousine?" It's okay to take a few minutes and jot down the math in your notebook. Bottom line: Be prepared for surprises and don't be afraid to ask for time to formulate your answer. Ultimately, in these situations it matters less what your answer to these curveball questions as much as you can showcase your poise, ability to think under pressure, and be creative. Work on ironing out your nerves, sounding comfortable and relaxed, and even the most zany question will be a breeze to answer.

Step 3: Hacking the Interview

This section is your playbook for slaying the interview so hard the hiring manager wants to cancel all other interviews. Many of these tips apply to both phone and in-person interviews, but there are a few extra stops you can pull out in person.

It's not just about your answers.

When hiring employees for client relations, my number-one reason for turning candidates down is lack of enthusiasm. If you sound bored during the phone interview, chances are, you're going to sound bored when you're on the phone with customers, and from a customer service standpoint, that's unacceptable. I've heard of this being the case at larger companies as well. If you're not enthusiastic about the job and you end up quitting three months down the road, the hiring manager will have some explaining to do with upper management. I'm not asking you to do cartwheels and act like you've won the lottery during the interview, but definitely don't sound like you've just woken up from a nap.

Hiring managers are looking for excuses *not* to hire you. It's their job to find the best candidates, so if you throw up any red flags, it's in their best interest *not* to give you the job.

Other Common Red Flags:

- Being late for the interview

- Being under-dressed

- Making it clear you didn't research the company

- Rambling/going off on tangents (If you get off track, it's okay to say, "I'm getting a little off track here. Would you repeat the question for me?")

- Being too self-centered (If all you talk about is how the position will benefit you, the interviewer may wonder if you're a team player.)

- Badmouthing previous employers (I don't care if your manager was arrested for embezzlement. Don't bad-mouth him or her.)

- Not being able to provide references from recent managers

- Lack of eye contact

- Job-hopping or large gaps in employment history

- Asking for things before you're even offered the job. "I can only work these days," or, "I have a vacation planned in June. Is that going to be an issue?" Don't jump the gun here. Wait until you are offered the position to have these conversations.

If you avoid these red flags, you've by default beat out some of the competition for the job. Throughout the interview, don't forget to actively engage in the conversation. Have a notebook out and write down any tidbits of information the interviewer gives you. You'll have practiced your answers and your delivery, so your interview will go off without a hitch.

Arrive and check in ten to fifteen minutes early. Bring a professional binder/report cover with your résumé, cover letter, letters of recommendation, portfolio, etc. When you meet the person or people conducting the interview, look them in the eye, smile, introduce yourself, and give a firm handshake.

Pro-Tip: Practice your handshake prior to the meeting with friends and family members. If your hand feels like Jell-O, it shows a lack of confidence and professional experience. Make it firm, not crushing. I've had an interviewee for a client relations position squeeze my hand like a boa constrictor. It hurt. To me, this showed a lack of social awareness, which is crucial for a client relations role.

Toward the end of the interview, you should ask the following questions:

- "How long have you been with the company?"

- "What do you love most about your job/working here?"

- "Tell me what I could expect on a day-to-day basis in this job."

- "I don't mean to put you on the spot, but I'd kick myself if I didn't ask this question: 'Do you have any reservations about my fit for this position that I can address right now?'"

- Next steps? (Oftentimes they'll give you this information without prompting.)

- Can I get your office mailing address? Is it ____? (give your best guess based on your previous research. It could be the building you're standing in. You'll need this to send a handwritten thank you card.)

A Powerful Combination: Eye Contact while Writing

Nod your head, make eye contact, and take notes during your final home run questions. The interviewer probably can't remember the last time their kid put their phone down and gave him or her their true undivided attention. Trust me, it'll make an impression.

End the interview with another firm handshake, a smile, and eye contact. Say something along the lines of, "Thank you for your time. I'm really excited by the opportunity and feel like this job is meant for me. What are the next steps? (If you haven't covered that already, of course.)"

After the interview, you shouldn't be worrying about whether or not your answers sounded good. The goal isn't to sound good; it's to sell the interviewer on why they should hire you and to show the interviewer you care about them and their company. If you've followed the previous steps, you've hit a home run.

Don't Be Afraid to Negotiate

My husband is an electrical engineer. At age twenty-six, he decided to switch firms. He had a few years of experience under his belt and followed my interview hacking advice to a tee. He nailed the interview and got an offer but wasn't thrilled with the number of vacation days they were giving him. So he called the hiring manager and said, "Thank you for the offer and this opportunity. Time off with family is really important to me, and at my previous job, I had seven extra vacation days. Is there any way you could match this for me?" They countered with three additional days and a $3,000 signing bonus, which he graciously accepted.

Don't be afraid to negotiate your starting salary, vacation days, or other benefits upfront. If you have multiple job offers, you can explain that another company is offering you X many more vacation days or X dollars more. Some companies won't budge, but many will. The worst they can say is no, and most people will be impressed with your boldness.

Boss's Action Plan:

1. Gather key information when you get the call or email to schedule the interview.

2. Do your homework and practice, practice, practice your interview responses until you nail them, while sounding genuine and conversational.

3. Arrive early and introduce yourself confidently, with a firm handshake, smile, and eye contact.

4. Bring a professional binder/report cover with your résumé, cover letter, letters of recommendation, portfolio, etc. Get a notebook and pen out so you can take notes throughout, especially when you ask questions at the end.

5. Don't worry about whether or not you sound good. Focus on selling yourself and showing the interviewer you care about them and their company. Show enthusiasm and a genuine interest.

6. Get your interviewer talking at the end. Actively listen and take notes while maintaining eye contact. The more you get them talking and show a genuine interest in what they have to say, the more they will like you.

7. When you get the offer, don't be afraid to negotiate.

In the next chapter, we'll discuss how bosses level up in the corporate world to earn bigger raises and faster promotions.

Chapter 7

Level Up In the Corporate World

Once you land the job, don't forget about the skills you touted in your interview. Employers picked you for a reason and will want to see these skills in the workplace. The goal isn't just to hack the interview—it's to hack the job itself and fast-track your success.

Work Harder and Smarter

Work hard. Go the extra 26.2 miles and make sure it shows in your work. Take on extra projects. Answer calls after-hours. Come in early and stay late. If you're given grunt work, knock it out with a smile on your face. If you want more challenging projects, ask your manager and coworkers if there's anything you can help them with. Are there any lingering projects or pressing deadlines you can help them meet?

Keep in mind, this stage won't last forever. You're a boss! This stage will go quicker the harder you work. Your coworkers may feel threatened, but don't dim your light just because it's too bright for someone else's eyes.

People may call you a brown-noser or try to make you feel bad for accomplishing at a higher level. Don't be offended. Don't pretend your work ethic isn't impressive, because it is. Smile and laugh it off, but don't discount yourself. You can still have very positive relationships with settlers and achievers in the workplace. Help a coworker meet a deadline and don't take any credit; make him or her a cup of coffee, just the way they like it. Go above and beyond to connect with your team, not just your superiors.

It Is Not a Competition, Even If It Is.

Are you and another achiever or boss vying for the same promotion? Do not fall into the trap of competing with this person. In fact, it may seem counterintuitive, but go out of your way to help them, give them credit, and show you care—even if they don't return the favor. Leaders create leaders and build people up. You will gain tremendous respect from the people around you if you take on this philosophy. And I don't know about you, but I believe what goes around comes around. (We'll discuss the Law of Attraction in a later chapter.)

Get to Know Your Manager.

What makes them happy? What stresses them out? Keep tabs on this for a week or two, jotting down events that provide insight into this. The goal is to identify their pain points so you can help relieve them.

During a performance review or scheduled meeting, pick your manager's brain. I'd recommend some of the following questions: "Please be honest with me. Is there anything I do that bothers you or stresses you out? What could I do in my role that would make your life easier? Is there anything else you would like to see more of from me? Anything you'd like to see less of? How can I be more of an asset to this company?" Now that your manager has given you the playbook, you can prove yourself in ways that count.

Keep tabs on yourself next. Are you coming to your manager with problems or solutions? Are you adding good energy to the room each time you interact, or are you leaving a bad vibe? As a manager, most of the things escalated to me are problems, but there is a huge difference in the approach of people with leadership potential and people without it. Here is a recent problem that was brought to my attention and two ways it could have been approached:

Lacking Leadership Potential	Leadership Potential
This client is being ridiculous. She expects me to call her all the time, even though I explained our policy is one monthly call. I told her I'd talk with my manager, but I just don't know how we're going to work with someone this needy.	This client was upset, so I heard her out and asked more questions so I could really understand where she's coming from. To make her happy, I really think we should touch base with her weekly instead of monthly. How do you feel about making an exception to our once-monthly call policy? If you're open to it, I'd like to run my plan of action for the next few weeks by you.

See what a difference that makes?

I've worked with multiple people who were fantastic employees, but avid complainers. I get the appeal. Venting feels good, and complaining about a shared problem can help you feel connected to those around you. While it may be tempting, do *not* use this as a strategy to connect with your manager. He or she may sympathize or provide constructive criticism to make you feel better, but chances are, they will leave the conversation feeling a bit drained. Do this on a regular basis and your manager will dread interacting with you. Consciously or subconsciously, they will see you as someone who drains their energy. When you have the urge to complain about a problem, flip the switch, create a solution, and come to your manager excited about your new idea.

Do everything you can to be more of an asset and make your manager happy. Eliminate anything you do (or fail to do) that stresses out your manager. Also, make sure your manager knows that you're happy in your current role but would love to move into a leadership position if given the opportunity.

Learn to Speak Your Manager's Language

Since taking the Core Values Index assessment I mentioned in chapter 4, I am now hyperaware of the people around me and their values. As a refresher, the core values are Builder (Power), Merchant (Love), Innovator (Wisdom), and Banker (Knowledge). Builders are so direct they can make others bristle after an interaction. Merchants in particular may think, "She didn't even take the time to ask how my day was—she just barged in and demanded I drop everything to help her." On the flip side, most Builders hate time-wasters. They want you to skip the pleasantries and get to the point. He or she may think, "Good grief, she spent ten minutes jabbering on about her day when I just needed a freaking signature."

If your manager is a Banker, you need to back up your claims. Let's say you implemented a new system that improved communication among your team. That will mean very little to a Banker unless it's backed up by measurable statistics that prove the team is operating more efficiently. If your manager is an Innovator, he or she loves to problem solve and likely values that ability in others. Brainstorming creative solutions and developing a vision can be a bonding experience with your manager. What language does your manager speak? How can you contribute in a way that is meaningful to his or her core values?

How to Make People Like You

A surefire way to make people like you is to make them feel important, because they are! You need your coworkers on your side if you plan to level up. On top of that, you never know who may be a connection for you five, ten, or twenty years down the road. And don't you want to make friends? Making friends is effortless if you show a genuine interest in getting to know your coworkers. In a John Maxwell leadership course I recently attended, we learned that to really connect with someone, you must know what makes them laugh, what makes them cry, and what they dream of doing or becoming. People love talking about themselves, so ask lots of questions and *really listen* to their answers without being mentally checked out. Learn what their interests are. For example, I'm obsessed with dogs, heavy metal, and the television show *The Office*. I simply can't help but like someone who strikes up an engaging conversation about any of these topics. What are your coworkers' obsessions?

Show enthusiasm when talking to people and make sure your body language communicates your interest. Science shows you should make eye contact, smile, point your feet in their direction, and lean in slightly when talking to them. *Just don't go overboard.* Staring into your coworker's soul without blinking could come off as creepy and aggressive.

Want to be a more interesting person? You don't need to tell better stories or funnier jokes. Simply be interested in others and get them talking about themselves. We *love* people who show an interest in us and will automatically see them as more interesting people too.

Make Choosing You a No-Brainer

Work so hard *and smart* that your manager feels obligated to give you a raise, and when a promotion is available, you are the clear choice. It should be a no-brainer. You've gone the extra marathon when everyone else went the extra mile. Your team would be lost without you!

Help Your Manager Help You

Do you want more flexibility? Time off? A higher salary? Know what you want so you can ask for it as you level up. If you're being rewarded with a promotion, it's important for your manager to understand what rewards mean most to you.

Boss's Action Plan

1. Write down three ways you will go the extra marathon at work this week.

2. Who is your biggest "competition" at work? Stop thinking of them as competition and start being their biggest supporter. How can you help this person succeed without taking credit?

3. Schedule a meeting, strike up a conversation with your manager, or simply pay more attention around the office. Write down five ways you can become more of a stress-reliever to your manager.

4. Take a CVI test and suggest the rest of the office takes one for more effective communication and collaboration.

5. Pay attention to the conversations you have at work. Are you constantly complaining, venting, or focusing the conversation on yourself? Make a conscious effort to talk less about you and get others to talk about themselves by asking open-ended questions.

6. Are you the clear choice for a promotion? If not, you haven't been going the extra marathon long enough or consistently enough. Write down two more ways you'll kick ass at work this week.

KEEP YOUR END GOAL IN MIND

Going the extra marathon isn't always feasible or fun. In later chapters, we'll discuss how to say no and master your time. For now, I want you to reassess your end goal. Is it bigger raises and faster promotions? A higher-level management or corporate-level position at your current company? If so, you believe your company is growing rapidly enough for fast-track advancement. Keep going the extra marathon.

Do you plan to use this job as a stepping stone to a bigger and better career within your field? If so, set a date for when you will start applying for higher-level jobs, or launch your own business. Put it on your calendar in stone. On this date, you will shift from going the extra marathon to just going the extra mile, so you can spend all excess time and energy applying, interviewing, and networking.

Is this job a way to make ends meet while you work on your book, business, or career in a brand new field? If you go the extra mile, instead of accepting a promotion, you could ask for more flexibility or time off. If you simply do what's required of you to allow maximum time and energy for your side hustle, you're not settling; you're being strategic. Either way, you can still do your work with a smile on your face.

Raises Don't Mean Riches

Raises, promotions, career moves, and side hustles don't guarantee you'll build wealth. Some people will *never* be rich no matter how much money they make, because the more they make, the more they'll spend. In the next chapter, I'll map out the path to seven figures and shed light on the poor money habits that will prevent a majority of college grads from ever reaching millionaire status.

Chapter 8

The Path to Seven Figures: Part 1

MILLIONAIRE MIND-SET

Do you believe you can become a millionaire? Or is it just some crazy fantasy to you? Think about this and answer honestly. I've always wanted to be a millionaire but never truly believed I would become one until my second year in business, when I was twenty-five years old.

As my bank account grew, one day it finally dawned on me that I could become a millionaire. I remember taking a long walk with my husband, going over the numbers, and getting so pumped up. Don't get me wrong: we were far off at this point, but we knew if we worked hard and got X number of clients, we could actually hit seven figures. We purposefully walked into the nicest neighborhood near us, looked at the big houses, and said, "*That's* where we're going to live."

Talk about motivation on steroids. I swear, in the following weeks, I became a different person. I started thinking big-picture. I identified my bottlenecks. I came up with a list of things I could outsource or hire someone else to handle and made it happen. I started focusing my efforts on my best clients and letting go of my headache ones. I took my business to the next level. And by the end of that year, I'd more than doubled my income.

This didn't come from a lucky break or a huge client. This came from a shift in my mentality. I went from disbelieving to believing I could become a millionaire, which gave me the motivation to make it happen.

Now, does a million dollars seem far-fetched to you? If so, you can start by developing the belief that 6-figures is possible first. I want to share a powerful resource I've created for you: 100 Money Affirmations I Used To Make 6-Figures (In Less Than 6 Months). You can download the affirmations in both print and audio formats, as well as access free wall prints and beautiful phone backgrounds with your favorite affirmations on them at: www.whycollegeisbroken.com/money. 6-Figures is a huge milestone on your path to a million dollars, and affirmations will help program your subconscious mind to develop the beliefs that you are worthy of becoming wealthy, capable of becoming wealthy, and that money is easy to come by. For affirmations to actually impact your subconscious mind, you must see and repeat them on a regular basis. This is why the affirmations for your wall and phone are so important.

Now, I want you to ask yourself the following questions:

- If you didn't believe you had a shot at being accepted into a sorority or fraternity, would you bother rushing?

- If you didn't think there was a chance you could pass a class, would you study hard for the exam?

- If you really didn't believe you could make the team, would you practice or even bother showing up at tryouts?

For most of us, we only try if we believe there's a good chance we can achieve something. Otherwise, we'd rather skip rush events, drop the class, or avoid tryouts altogether. The same applies to wealth. If you don't believe there's a realistic chance you could earn a million dollars, you won't become rich. I'm not saying you won't try to make money; you simply won't try at a level needed to actually earn seven figures.

Let's say you just graduated college and hear of an amazing job opportunity. It pays close to six figures and is in your dream field. The problem is, it requires five years more experience than you have.

A settler, who doesn't believe she has a snowball's chance in hell of becoming a millionaire, thinks, "Eh, I'm not even going to bother applying. I don't have the experience. There's no way I'll get the job."

An achiever, who hopes to be rich one day but doesn't *fully* buy into the concept of actually earning a million dollars, thinks, "Maybe I'll apply. I'm a hard worker. I probably won't get the job, but it's worth a shot."

A boss, who wholeheartedly believes they are going to become a millionaire and is looking for opportunities at every turn, thinks, "Hey, this could be the first step toward my dream career. I'm going to apply, add the hiring manager on LinkedIn, and submit a video résumé explaining why I'm the perfect candidate for this position, despite my lack of industry experience. I'm going to do *whatever it takes* to get their attention. If they don't give me the job, maybe the people I meet will be a connection for me down the road."

After all, if you don't believe in you, why should anyone else?

You've Got to Live in a Millionaire Mind-set

Now, I want you to take a second and think about your relationship with money. What does wealth mean to you? Do you buy into phrases like, "Money is the root of all evil," or, "Money doesn't buy happiness"? When you think of a rich person, what words would you use to describe them? If words like "greedy" or "snob" come to mind, you are not living in a millionaire mind-set. This negative attitude toward money will prevent you from earning it. If you are jealous of millionaires and are hating on successful people, that breeds negativity, which, simply put, makes you feel bad. Feeling bad prevents you from taking action. And it takes action to earn a million dollars.

The same thing goes for saying things like, "I'm so poor," or, "I'm so broke." Say it enough and you'll convince yourself it's true. Convince yourself it's true, and you won't take action at the level needed to actually make seven figures.

A huge percentage of our population will never be rich no matter how much money they make. The more they make, the more they'll spend. These are the settlers of the world, or, unfortunately, achievers who have the financial savvy of settlers. See the chart below. The first step on the path to seven figures is awareness of your bad financial habits, so you can change them.

Signs You'll Always Be Poor (Settlers)	Signs You'll Be Comfortable (Achievers)	Signs You'll Be Rich (Bosses)
You live above your means.	You live within your means.	You live below your means.
You believe credit cards allow you to get the things you want when you want them, regardless of your income. Making the minimum payments each month allows you the financial flexibility you need.	You use your credit card when you have to and try to pay it off when you can. Sometimes, you let the interest build when you can't afford to pay it down.	You either don't use credit cards, or pay them off regularly so you don't waste a penny in interest payments.
Saving an emergency fund isn't necessary. That's what credit cards and friends are for.	Saving a small emergency fund is important.	Saving an emergency fund equivalent to three to six months of income is non-negotiable.
You agree with the statement "Debt is a part of life."	You aim to minimize debt but leverage it occasionally when you can't afford something.	You fiercely eliminate debt.
You don't even consider investing.	You dabble with investing, but nothing too serious.	You develop an investment portfolio with the help of an expert so you can make money while you sleep.
Your job is your only source of income, which may or may not be steady.	Your job is a healthy source of steady income.	You have multiple streams of income, which multiplies your earning potential.
You don't save for retirement. Life is short! You'd	You may save some money for retirement, but may or may not utilize	You always fully utilize the employee contribu-

Signs You'll Always Be Poor (Settlers)	Signs You'll Be Comfortable (Achievers)	Signs You'll Be Rich (Bosses)
rather spend that money while you're young.	the employee contribution match at work.	tion match at work because it's free money. Whenever possible, you max out your retirement contributions.
You buy brand names and designer items that make you look rich, regardless of whether or not you can afford them.	You buy brand names and designer items that you can afford, but you could put that money to better use (i.e., an extra student loan or car payment).	You care more about being rich than looking rich. You wait until you're out of debt, then purchase brand names and designer items in cash, or not at all. Have you ever seen the late Steve Jobs? He wore plain T-shirts and jeans on the regular.
Your financial know-how allows you to scrape by. You know how to keep your electricity from being shut off and keep your bank account from going negative before your next paycheck (most of the time.)	You acquired a baseline of financial skills before or during early adulthood, but the learning stopped there.	You are committed to learning new ways to improve your financial situation and aren't afraid to bring in an expert for guidance. You will find a way to become rich no matter what.

Which category most describes you? If you're an achiever, you're one step away from transforming your financial life. Mostly a settler? I love a good comeback story.

Now that you understand the mind-set necessary to become wealthy, we'll discuss the danger of debt and the importance of taking massive action to get out of it.

Chapter 9

The Path to Seven Figures: Part 2

THE DANGER OF DEBT

Debt is one of your worst financial enemies. Think of it as a leech that latches on to your bank account and sucks money out slowly over time via interest payments. How many leeches do you want on your bank account?

I want you to do a quick exercise. Pull up your latest student loan or credit card bill. Find the line that says "Interest Payment" and mentally cross it out with a fat red marker, replacing it with the words "Money I Am Throwing Away." Now, really let that sink in. That is *your* money. You could've used it to save up for a vacation or a new car. You could've gone shopping with it. You could've put it towards your retirement or some other investment that would allow you to make money while you sleep. But instead, you willingly gave it to that bloodthirsty leech (or lender). It seems ludicrous, doesn't it?

Lenders make a *fortune* off settlers. Settlers either ignore or accept the fact that they're in debt and probably always will be. Each month when they pay their interest payments, they'll stare those fat leeches in their swollen faces and shrug, "Nothing I can do about it. Debt is a part of life."

According to an article by the Pew Research Center's Fact Tank, only 27 percent of young college graduates with student loans self-report that they are living comfortably—note, these 27 percent are not claiming to be rich.[13] They are simply living *comfortably*. I don't know about you, but when I went to college, I expected "living comfortably" afterwards would be a given. Additionally, 21 percent of adults aged eighteen to twenty-nine who held at least a bachelor's degree and had outstanding student loans held more than one job, and only 51 percent of college graduates with student loans say that they believe that the lifetime benefits of their degrees outweigh the costs.[14]

If this is starting to freak you out, you can at least know that you're not alone. A report compiled by the US Department of Education reports that the national student loan debt burden rose to over $1.2 trillion in May of 2013.[15] While there are the occasional outliers who have borrowed exorbitant amounts—including an orthodontist in Utah who has taken out over $1 million in student loans—the average student loan amount according to the US Department of Education is only $26,946.[16]

$26,946 doesn't seem like too much, right? $26,946 may be roughly equivalent to the price of a mid-level new car, but it comes nowhere close to the price of a new home, so if this is all the debt you have, you should be in good shape, right? Unfortunately, that isn't how debt works. This may all start to sound like the student loan exit counseling you had to do before graduating college, but I ask that you all bear with me here, because this is important: all loans, by nature, come with interest. Loans without interest are essentially gifts, and the federal government and private lenders would really have no incentive to give them to you; they would just be letting you use their money without getting anything in return. Because of this, your student loans, regardless of who you are lending from, will accrue interest until you pay them off. According to the US Department of Education, the average interest rate for federal student loans is 3.9 percent.[17] This interest rate can be even higher if you take out loans from private banks and institutions instead of from the government. Of course, no interest is good interest, but you can cut down on how much of your money you are throwing away by repaying your loans as quickly as possible. But with the most recent generations of college grads, that doesn't seem to be happening. Based on data gathered by the US Department of Education on students who graduated college in the 2007–2008 school year, only 69 percent of respondents were actively repaying their student loans, and only 17 percent of those respondents had totally paid off their student loans. Nine percent of those polled were not making payments on their debt at all, and 5 percent had defaulted. Perhaps most startling of all, 24 percent of respondents had at least one delinquent loan, meaning they had missed at least one payment. All of this means that most recent college grads aren't making the timely payments necessary to keep their interest under control. This can result in payment periods lasting 175 months (about 14.5 years) or more. While these longer repayment periods may make your individual payments smaller, it means that ultimately you are going to be paying more over time. So your seemingly manageable $26,946 student loan can balloon into $35,612 over that 175-month repayment period, meaning that you will be paying nearly $10,000 in interest.

If you have student loans, you can't go back and unborrow, but you can pay them back as quickly as possible. Depending on your interest rates and repayment period, you could end up paying close to double your original loan amount, especially if you utilize forbearance and deferment. I know people who have borrowed over $100,000 in student loans and could end up paying close to $200,000 when it's all said and done. In fact, going off of averages for interest rates and starting salaries for college, my friend with $100,000 in student loans could end up paying $188,877 in total, which is nearly $90,000 in interest alone. What if they could've kept that $90,000 in interest payments and used it to make a down payment on a house? Or took a year off work to travel the world, all expenses paid?

Removing the Leeches

So you've got your student loan leech, your car leech, credit card leech(es). And if you haven't already purchased your first home, you may soon find yourself with a mortgage leech. Some leeches are worse than others, so let's break down the different types of debt and which ones you should eliminate first. When I talk about elimination, I mean living like a poor college kid, even if you have a full-time salaried job, so you can make double or triple payments to pay down your debt. I'm a big fan of the book *Total Money Makeover* by Dave Ramsey. You'll notice many of my recommendations fall in line with Dave's teachings because they work—I know from personal experience. More importantly, I've seen firsthand how the settlers I know have gotten themselves into a debt quicksand. With poor money habits, they've found it nearly impossible to pull themselves out.

1. Payday Loans

Payday loans market themselves as solutions for people who are strapped on cash to get them by until their next paycheck. I consider it stealing from the poor. These loans have exorbitant interest rates, ranging from 300 percent to more than 500 percent APR. If you've taken a payday loan, pay it off ASAP and never take one out again.

2. Credit Card Debt

Credit cards have notoriously high interest rates, around 15 percent or more. Let's say you've racked up $3,000 in credit card debt. If you make minimum payments of $60 at a 15 percent interest rate, you will be paying $36 in interest every month and $24 towards your balance. At this rate, it will take you sixteen years to pay off a $3,000 balance, and you will pay a total of

$6,641. Chances are, whatever you spent $3,000 on will be forgotten, lost, or broken by then!

After you knock out any outstanding payday loans, pull out all the stops to pay off your credit card balance. Then, continue to pay off the balance every month or cut up your card if you don't have the financial discipline to do so.

3. Student Loans, Car Debt & Any Other Personal Debt

There is some debate about which leech you should rip off next. Dave Ramsey recommends paying off whatever leech has the smallest balance, so you can build momentum. He calls it the "debt snowball." I have found this strategy to be extremely motivating. However, one could argue you should pay off whatever leech has the highest interest rate. Feel out whatever method works best for you.

How to Remove the Student Loan Leech:

(Part 1) If You're Still in College ...	(Part 2) Once You've Graduated ...
Live below your means.	Live below your means.
Apply for as many scholarships as possible.	Start paying your loan payments before your grace period is over. This is a period of time where your loans aren't building interest, so your payments make a bigger impact at reducing your overall debt.
Work as much as you can in the summer and during school to save up so you can take as few loans as possible.	The lower your monthly payment, the longer your repayment period. So the less you pay every month, the more you will pay in interest throughout the life of the loan. Take the shortest repayment period and the highest monthly payment.
If you decide to take a loan, search for loans with the lowest interest rates you can find. Below 4 percent is ideal.	Work overtime or start a side hustle so you can make double or triple payments to pay down your debt fast.

4. Mortgage Debt

This is typically your fattest leech and the most difficult to remove, so you'll tackle it last. This leech sucks on your bank account for fifteen to thirty years, usually longer for most Americans, because as soon as they can afford a bigger leech, they "move up" in the world.

Did You Know Rent Itself Can Be a Leech?

Renting long-term is terrible for your financial situation because you don't build equity. Your payments help your landlord pay off a property they own and can eventually sell for cash. Buy a house, and any money you pay towards principle is *your* money (i.e., your down payment and the portion of your monthly payment that doesn't go towards insurance or interest).

But Renting Isn't Always Bad, Especially for College Grads

Don't make the mistake of jumping into homeownership if you aren't sure where you want to live or who you want to live with long-term. Moving in a year or two? Just rent. During your first year or two as a homeowner, aside from your down payment, your monthly payments make a negligible impact on principle. You'll pay realtor fees, title fees, and insurance. Mortgage interest is front-loaded, so you could make a $1,000 mortgage payment with only $150 of it going towards the principle. Now, if your air conditioner goes out or a pipe bursts, you could go in the hole. And what if the market tanks? You could have trouble selling, or worse, have to sell your home for less than the original purchase price. The market could go up and you could make money, but if you're only going to live in the house for a year or two, it's not worth the gamble.

How to Remove the Mortgage Leech

- Save as much as possible for a down payment, at least 10 percent. (20% is ideal. The closer you can get to 100 percent, the better!)

- Opt for the fifteen-year mortgage. If you can't afford the payment, buy a smaller house. Thirty-year mortgages will cost you tens of thousands more in interest.

- Aim for keeping your mortgage payment below one-third of your income.

- Once you've removed your other leeches, take all the money you would be spending on your car, student loans, or other debt and start chipping away at your house debt. Make an extra payment whenever you can. We'll talk in later chapters about starting a business, moving up in a fast-growing company, and pursuing your dream career, so you can eventually make double, triple, or even ten times the monthly payment until you're living in a paid-off home.

Living below your means is non-negotiable for getting out of debt. If you have to borrow to buy something, you can't afford it (with the exception of a house). Understanding this is the first step. The next step is to fiercely cut your expenses so you can throw as much money as possible towards your debt.

For the next week or two, I want you to keep a notebook with you at all times and track every single penny you spend. We're not always consciously aware of the money we're spending. Have you ever driven home at night and suddenly you end up in your driveway wondering how you got there? You were on autopilot, making the familiar turns, so much so that an entire car ride feels like a blur. We do this with spending money too! Maybe you drive by Starbucks every morning for a $5 coffee or head to a local bistro for a $12 salad at lunch. These purchases may seem harmless and easy to justify for anyone who doesn't understand the time value of money. In the book *The Compound Effect* by Darren Hardy, he explains that if you invest $1 today at an 8 percent interest rate, it is worth almost $5 in twenty years and $10 in thirty years. So that $5 coffee you purchased this morning just took $25 off your future bank balance. That salad is costing you $60 in twenty years and $120 in thirty years. Let's say you purchase that salad three times a week for five years. Thirty years later, you will have cost yourself a whopping $93,600.

That's a little harder to stomach, isn't it? Buy ground coffee in bulk and your own bag of lettuce. Your future self will thank you.

Investing before You're out of Debt

You may be thinking, "Okay, Chelsea, if I can make an 8 percent return on my investment and my interest rate on my student loans is 5 percent, shouldn't I invest instead of pay down my debt?" Great question. I've met many financially savvy folks who would argue yes. Invest and yield the higher return. There are many millionaires who have earned their wealth by taking risks, investing, and going further into debt. But personally, I despise the idea of purchasing a cash cow when I still have multiple leeches sucking my bank account dry. What if disaster strikes? The market tanks? You lose your job? You get cancer? You have to drain your investment accounts just to pay the bills? If you've got a mortgage, car loan, student loans, and credit card debt, those bills will be crippling. For me, paying off debt is like purchasing peace of mind.

Get with a financial advisor to determine when you should start investing. I recommend everyone invest in a retirement account. Some are more tax-favorable than others, so do your research or speak with your advisor to determine which option is best for you.

As I said before, always fully utilize the employee contribution match at work because it's *free money*. And once you're out of debt, put as much money as you can towards retirement every year, maxing out the contributions whenever possible.

How to Live Like a Broke College Kid

Once you've tracked your expenses for a couple of weeks, you will find areas of unnecessary overspending that can likely be drastically cut or eliminated altogether. As Dave Ramsey always says, "If you live like no one else, later you can live like no one else." Therefore, your goal should be to live like a broke college kid after graduation until you're out of debt. Most graduates get a taste of that full-time salary and start spending like they're rich. Because of this, paradoxically, they will live most of their adult lives broke as those debt leeches suck them dry.

Living like a broke college kid is easy. If you recently graduated, chances are, you're already used to it!

- Create a shoestring budget and stick to it.

- Clip coupons.

- Live off beans and rice.

- Shop at the bulk aisle in the grocery store.

- Shop at consignment stores and buy used items whenever possible.

- Bow out of expensive weekend plans with your friends.

- Hold off on taking that vacation.

- Cut up your credit cards if you don't have the discipline to pay them off before they build interest.

- Pay for things in cash so you can physically see the money you are spending and feel that pit in your stomach when you overspend.

- Work overtime or start a side hustle so you can make double or triple payments to pay down your debt fast.

The more disciplined you are, the quicker you will build wealth. That being said, don't beat yourself up if you mess up, and know that it's okay to treat yourself every now and then. My husband and I got in the habit of celebrating our debt payments. When we made a big payment towards our debt, we'd celebrate with a fancy dinner. We splurged on the celebrations each time we paid off a loan with shopping trips, weekend getaways, and beach vacations. Now that we're living debt free, we splurge on luxuries whenever we feel like it, while still living below our means.

Living like you're broke to eliminate debt puts you on the fast-track to seven figures, but more importantly, buys you the flexibility and freedom to take risks, pursue your passions, and build your dream life. When opportunity knocks, you'll be in the position to open the door. You'll have the money to invest in that start-up, the ability to quit your job to raise your kids, start that novel, or launch a company.

Living below your means does *not* mean you have to live with a scarcity mind-set. Instead of focusing on all the things you can't buy, focus on all the ways you can save now so you can splurge later. Get in the habit of telling yourself, "I'm going to be *so* rich." Visualize all the incredible places you'll be able to travel to and all the once-in-a-lifetime experiences you'll be able to afford. Picture that shopping spree in vivid detail. Visualize that paid-off car or boat sitting in the driveway of your mansion. My husband and I did this so frequently that saving and paying off debt became exciting for us. Living below your means can be enjoyable if you keep the end goal in mind instead of focusing on what you can't have now.

What's the Opposite of a Leech?

An income stream is the opposite of a leech. Income streams feed your bank account instead of sucking it dry. The secret to becoming a millionaire is to live like you're broke and rip off your leeches while developing multiple income streams, then working to make those income streams bigger and bigger, until eventually, you're making money in your sleep. In the next chapter, I'll demystify that process.

Chapter 10

The Path to Seven Figures: Part 3

MULTIPLE INCOME STREAMS

It's been said that the average millionaire has seven streams of income. I currently have five: my business, speaking engagements, consulting work, a commercial office building, and kickbacks from referring clients who need services outside of our realm to other marketing firms. Unfortunately, our education system primes us to plan for one source of income from the moment we graduate until we retire: our jobs.

Now, I'm not saying jobs are a bad thing. Our society needs jobs, and entrepreneurs need jobs to build businesses. Entrepreneurship is not for everyone. Some people are happier in steady jobs and that's perfectly fine, but it doesn't mean they can't develop another stream of income.

Putting all of your eggs in the job basket is dangerous. What if you get fired or laid off? What if a new technology makes your job obsolete? What if you're miserable? What if that career you were so excited to pursue ends up feeling soul-sucking, or your coworkers are assholes, or your manager sucks?

Losing your primary source of income could be life-shattering, but it doesn't have to be. The more streams of income you develop and the larger those streams become, the less you have to rely on your job.

An income stream is anything that feeds your bank account. It can be a job, side gig, real estate, book, or business, to name a few. In section 2, we'll focus on launching a business, so for now, I'll focus on other ways to diversify your income.

Passive Income

Passive income is income you earn without active involvement in the venture after the initial setup. For example, if you own property and rent it out, the rent check you receive every month is passive income. I'm not saying you won't have to maintain the property, but your income isn't tied to how many hours you work. Hire a maintenance person and maid service when a tenant moves out to minimize time invested.

When developing multiple income streams, millionaires often favor passive streams because the time commitment is minimal, especially if they hire people to manage their affairs. The goal is to put cash flow on autopilot so you can make money while you sleep.

Now, I realize most college grads don't have the money to invest in a rental property or hire help, so here are a few ways you can make (mostly) passive income with little to no cash up front:

Start house and pet sitting.

You can literally get paid while you sleep by watching someone's home or furry friend while they're out of town.

Get a roommate, or rent out an unused room via Airbnb.com.

This is a great way to lower rent costs or make additional income. If you want to minimize time invested with the Airbnb, hire a maid via Care.com.

Rent your car for ad space.

Carvertise.com is a simple way to make money while you drive.

Sell stock photos.

You can use websites such as Alamy.com, Shutterstock.com, or Adobe Stock at stock.adobe.com.

Become a social influencer.

Influencers are people who have the clout to influence large numbers of people and impact purchasing decisions via social or traditional media. Start a blog, vlog (video blog), and/or podcast and build your following on social media. Find your niche and create high-quality, authentic content that really speaks to this audience. There are entire books on building your audience and making money as an influencer. Apps like Muses and Collabor8 are an easy way to connect with brands who may want to pay or provide free merchandise in exchange for promotion on your social channels.

You can create your own merch, such as T-shirts or ebooks, host events, and drive traffic to your website, which can be monetized via platforms like AdSense by Google. AdSense allows you to make money by letting brands run ads on your website. Becoming an influencer can fast-track the success of your career or business. We'll discuss this further in Chapter 17.

Leverage investment apps.

There are tons of apps which allow you to invest your money quickly and easily. Here are a few to get you started:

Learn: How to invest in stocks is pretty self-explanatory. If you're new to investing, I'd highly recommend Learn.

Acorns allows you to automatically invest your spare change from purchases by linking it to your credit or debit account.

SigFig acts as an online investment advisor, allowing you to create a diversified financial portfolio for a fraction of the cost of traditional financial advisors.

Fundrise is an alternative to investing in the stock market. For as little as $500, you can invest in private market real estate and diversify your portfolio.

Write a book or song.

After the upfront work of writing a book or song, you can earn royalties without lifting a finger. For songs, sites like TuneCore.com allow you to easily sell your music online. For books, Amazon's CreateSpace.com allows you to independently publish your book for free. Of course, the more you market yourself and your brand, the more you'll sell.

Create an online store and drop ship products.

Drop shipping allows you to sell products without physically carrying inventory. Therefore, you move products from the manufacturer directly to the end consumer. If you go this route, you have to find a trustworthy supplier, get your profit margins in check, and find a platform to sell on that consumers trust. I know so many people who tried to build their own website and sell to consumers, only to find that consumers didn't trust or want to buy from their no-name brand. Do your research before you dive into this space.

Create an online course.

Everyone is an expert at something. Think about your strengths and your experience. Do you have skills or knowledge that would benefit others? The key to winning in this space is to find a niche and create hyper-unique content that speaks to this audience. Social media marketing is foundational to the success of your course, and becoming an influencer will massively increase your chance of making a profit.

Multi-Level Marketing (MLM) Businesses

I have a love-hate relationship with multi-level marketing (MLM) businesses. I know a handful people who have earned five or six figures through MLM. However, I know hundreds, and through the grapevine thousands, of people who buy into the excitement of starting their own business but at the end of the day, after all the training, parties, events, and social media promotion, they're barely making minimum wage.

I'm not saying getting rich with MLM is impossible, but it's an uphill battle and the market is saturated. Your involvement may also create an awkward tension in your relationships if your growth strategy relies heavily on selling to friends and family members. If you go the MLM route, find a unique product that sells itself and has resources for those who don't want to sell to friends and family, or be a boss and start your own MLM business.

Your second stream of income doesn't have to be passive. You could provide professional consulting services or build websites. You could create artwork, build furniture, mow lawns, or pressure wash decks. I'll provide a longer list of business ideas in the next chapter, but you get the picture. When you have the means, you may choose to invest in real estate, startups, or other ventures that require a heftier financial commitment.

What will life be like when you don't have to pay rent or a mortgage every month? What will you do with this newfound freedom?

Will you travel the world? Go on a shopping spree? Buy that car you've always wanted? Switch careers? Go back to school to study something you're passionate about? Become a stay-at-home parent? Write a book? Invent that product or develop that app? Finally go after your dream of being an actor, musician, athlete, or artist? Start a charity or fulfill some other philanthropic calling? Develop a vision for your debt-free life and use it as motivation. Visualize that life every day as you pack your own lunch and pass by Starbucks. With enough discipline, the possibilities for your life are truly limitless.

Boss's Action Plan:

1. Live like a poor college kid until you eliminate all debt leeches.

2. Commit to always living below your means, even as your income grows.

3. Save an emergency fund equivalent to three to six months of income.

4. Create another income stream completely separate from your day job.

5. Focus on making your income stream bigger and, if possible, self-sustaining before you move onto the next stream. The more you can put on autopilot, the more time and energy you'll have to invest in the next stream.

6. When you have the financial means, consider investing in real estate, stocks, startups, or other ventures with the guidance of a trusted financial advisor.

7. Nurture your streams or continue creating new streams until your income matches your vision for your life, goals, and dreams.

Chapter 11

Launching a Business

In a job, you're trading your time for a paycheck to make someone else rich. Want to go on vacation? Hope you have enough PTO. Want to make more money? Hope your position doesn't have a salary cap. Bosses feel suffocated by this lack of freedom and therefore will do whatever it takes to diversify their income and break free from the corporate world. They'll work all day at their job and all night on their craft or business because the idea of being told what to do and where to do it for eight-plus hours a day until retirement is unbearable.

When you think about working full-time for *someone else* now until you retire, how does it make you feel? Suffocated? Depressed? Pissed off? Awesome. Let's venture into the world of entrepreneurship.

One of my main inspirations for writing this book was the fact that I graduated with a business degree and nearly $30,000 in debt, yet I had *no clue* how to actually start a business. You'd think this would be Business 101, a necessity to understand before you graduate, but you'd be wrong. I could tell you the definition of a sole proprietorship versus an LLC versus an S-Corp, but if you had asked me how to actually start one, I'd stare at you like a deer in headlights.

Moreover, simply knowing *how* to start a business is not enough. You must develop the skill-set and mind-set to be successful as a business owner, which is rarely taught in school. Before I get into the how, I'm going to ask you to give yourself a hard reality check. Now is the time to identify your weaknesses. Look in the mirror and be brutally honest with yourself about your ability to connect with others, your attitude, your work ethic, and your accountability. I want you to take this quick quiz to determine how ready you are to start a company. Write or mentally note how the following statements apply to you, using strongly agree, agree, neutral, disagree, or strongly disagree.

- I consider myself a good communicator.

- I connect well with others.

- I have the ability to get other people to open up to me.

- I make a conscious effort to be positive.

- I make a point to be honest with others, even when it's not what they want to hear.

- I do not consider myself a people pleaser.

- I follow through on my word.

- I consistently meet or exceed deadlines.

- I show up early.

- I stay up late to get important things done.

- I rarely complain. I focus on being grateful for the good things in my life instead of complaining about the negative things.

- When things don't go my way, I don't blame others or the world. I ask myself what I could've done better and commit to doing it better next time.

- When I make mistakes, I learn from the experience and move past them as quickly as possible.

- I take responsibility for my emotions. I am aware of them and leverage willpower to my advantage.

If you said strongly disagree or disagree with any of the above statements, commit to self-improvement in those areas. You may consider getting a partner who excels in your areas of weakness, but the best-case scenario would be to work on yourself until you can strongly agree, or at least agree, with all of the above statements. You won't always live up to these statements perfectly, but they should feel more true than false. Here are some helpful resources:

- To improve connection and communication skills: *How to Win Friends and Influence People* by Dale Carnegie

- To improve work ethic and accountability: *The 10 Times Rule* by Grant Cardone

- To improve your attitude and leadership abilities: *The Difference Maker: Making Your Attitude Your Greatest Asset* by John Maxwell

When I started my business, I was a habitually late, brownnosing, people pleaser who was terrified of confronting people with bad news. Because of this, my first few years in business were extremely stressful. Refer back to the CVI assessment we took in chapter 4. Identify where your weak points are so you can either improve or work around them. Eventually, you will hire people to delegate your weaknesses to, so you can focus on your strengths.

Once you've got the skill-set and mind-set to be successful in the business world, decide what business you want to start. Don't get caught up perfecting your logo and business name until you answer these important questions.

Will you sell a product or service? What problems will your product or service solve? What will you do differently from everyone else in the market? And what will you do better?

Think about these questions long and hard. Can you create a more affordable solution? A higher-quality solution? A quicker solution? Get crystal clear on what will set you apart and know your success will boil down to how much value you bring to the market. What can you do better than your competitors to add value to your potential customers' lives?

As companies experience growing pains, quality often takes a backseat. Since I started Creekmore Marketing, I've been competing with gargantuan internet marketing firms with hundreds of people on staff and seemingly endless resources. How in the world was a college grad with minimal experience going to compete with companies like that?

It's simple, really. I did my research and identified my ideal customers' pain points. I asked every small business owner I came across what pisses them off about working with these big companies. I heard two resounding answers: "They suck, but they've got me locked into a year-long contract so I'm stuck. And they are working with two of my competitors in town. Our ads look almost exactly the same!"

So I implemented a no long-term contract policy. I told potential customers that we planned to keep them around by growing their business, not by locking them into a contract, and if their sales didn't increase, I fully expected them to fire me. I instantly earned trust and huge brownie points.

Then, I promised them that if they signed up for our SEO program, we wouldn't work with any of their competitors in town for a few reasons: (1) It wouldn't be fair. How can you expect to be successful with the same strategy as your competitors? And (2) To really market their business effectively, we needed to learn it inside and out. Our exclusivity policy allows our customers to feel safe sharing their secret sauce with us.

I can't tell you how many people I met in my first two years who told me that offering exclusivity was the wrong move. I remember one time in particular where a consultant in my business networking group pulled me aside and said, "I've been a business coach for twenty years and I think you're making a huge mistake with your exclusivity policy. You're pigeonholing yourself. I would seriously reconsider it if you want to grow."

Thank goodness I trusted my gut and didn't give up on the policy. Sure, I've turned away tens of thousands of dollars in business because I can't work with two clients in the same town, but I've gained ten times that in recurring revenue from long-term customers. Not only was it easier to sell these customers in the first place because of our exclusivity policy, but they were incentivized to stay with us. Whenever a competitor tried to hire us, I'd let the client know by saying, "Hey, ABC Lawncare reached out and tried to hire us. Of course I turned them away, but I wanted to let you know they are looking into marketing strategies. I will keep a close eye on them for you."

What pain points can become your value propositions?

If competition is steep in the industry you want to venture into, remember that being better than your competitors often boils down to customer service. There are tons of people out there doing what you want to do, but cutting corners, forgetting to follow up, missing deadlines, or pissing people off with their terrible interpersonal skills. This stuff isn't rocket science. If you're a hard worker and committed to doing right by your customers, you will naturally excel in this department. When I started my business, even though I didn't have the experience, resources, or staff of some of these bigger companies, I was able to set myself apart through dedication and top-notch customer service.

Maybe your unique positioning is clear, or maybe you have no clue. Regardless, it's important to create a customer profile and understand it inside and out. Ask yourself the following questions:

- Will you sell to the end consumer (Business to Consumer/B2C) or to another business (Business to Business/B2B)?

- What type of person buys your product or service?

- How old are they?

- Where do they live?

- Where do they work?

- How much money do they make?

- What are their hobbies and interests?

- What is important to them?

- What pisses them off?

- What feelings motivate them to buy?

Once you understand your target customer, you must adjust your product or service until your sales pitch is a *slam dunk* to them.

Finding a Niche

If your offering still falls flat, consider going after a niche. When I started my business, competition was ridiculously steep because anyone could claim they were an "internet marketing guru." The barrier to entry was practically nonexistent—anyone with a computer and internet connection could start a bedroom internet marketing firm. I was competing against huge companies who had gotten greedy or found themselves amid so much corporate red tape, they were unable to adapt as the internet marketing space evolved. On the flip side, I was competing against amateurs sitting in their underwear, living in their parents' basements, pretending to be "experts." Because of this, *so* many business owners had been burned. I didn't just have to convince them to buy into our brand, I had to convince them to buy into internet marketing as a whole. This alone could've put me out of business, but it didn't, because I found my niche: window treatments.

The window treatment industry was familiar to me because I'd worked in my family's business throughout high school and college. Once I chose this niche, my marketing materials and sales pitches were *slam dunks* because I knew how to resonate with window treatment dealers. I could talk their lingo; I had experience scheduling appointments, creating quotes, and closing sales. I could empathize with their struggles, because I'd watched my father go through them my entire life. I knew their profit margins and which products they most wanted to sell. Because of this, potential clients trusted that my marketing approach would be customized and effective.

People in the industry learned my story and started to spread the word. I created a few case studies from my first handful of clients and we went viral. Instead of cold calling these dealers, they were referred and would contact me. Oftentimes, they were halfway sold before I even got them on the phone. What niches can you serve?

Gaining Niche Experience

If you don't have the experience I did, go out and get it. You can interview people in the industry, shadow them, or even better, apply for a job. I worked in my family's window treatment business for five years, but it's not like I'm getting bonus points with my clients for that fourth and fifth year. In fact, no one *ever* asks how long I worked there. Study your industry intensively, interview people with experience, and you can become an expert faster than you ever expected.

The Unattainable Triangle: Time, Price, Quality

If it's fast and cheap, it's not good.
If it's cheap and good, it's not fast.
If it's good and fast, it's not cheap.

Okay, so this is something I *did* learn in business school. When positioning yourself in the market, you may only pick two of the three in the unattainable triangle. To pick all three is bad business. If you've got an awesome product, why discount it? If your turnaround time is lightning fast, why charge the same amount as competitors who are slower?

In the minds of consumers, price equals quality. (Regardless of whether this is actually the case.) Therefore, if you try to sell a widget for half the price of everyone else, people will think, "What's wrong with it? They must've cut corners somewhere."

At Creekmore Marketing, we are fast and good, but not cheap. I tried to be cheap in the beginning and actually had customers tell me I should charge more next time. I was selling good websites for $600 a pop and turning them around in a week or two. I quickly became overloaded and realized at that price point, the business was not scalable. Many new business owners make the mistake of pricing their products or services way too low. This is fine for your first few jobs to develop your portfolio and get some testimonials, but it will put you out of business long-term if you're also faster and better than your competition.

How to Start a Business

Now, I'm going to walk you through how to start a business step-by-step in the United States. (There are plenty of online resources if you live outside the United States!) The best advice I can give you is don't drag this process out. Many entrepreneurs will spend weeks, months, or even years agonizing over the perfect business name or nitpicking the logo. To be successful as a business owner, you must get obsessed with action over perfection. Start your journey today and adjust your sails later, or risk sitting on the shore next to all the other woulda-been, coulda-beens. Logos and branding can be revamped. Business names can be changed. (In fact, there is a really quick "doing business as" form you can fill out to operate under a different name than your legal business name.)

Step 1. Develop a laser-focused vision for your business. You already know your target audience and their pain points, so now you must decide how you want to sell to them. If you're selling products, will you have a supplier or manufacture your own products? If you're providing a service, will you provide it yourself, or do you plan to outsource or hire? Will customers purchase from you once or repeatedly?

"But Chelsea, shouldn't I create an official business plan?" Maybe. If your business requires a heavy investment up front, you'll definitely want to create a formalized business plan to help you think through every possible scenario and determine if your investment is likely to yield a worthwhile return. Preferably for your first business, you'll choose an industry that requires minimal investment so you have the freedom to experiment with your first customers and discover how your business will be profitable. To start Creekmore Marketing, all I needed was a computer and an internet connection. Here are some things you can become with little to no investment up front: marketer, social media manager, virtual assistant or secretary, bookkeeper, travel concierge, eBay seller, Etsy shop owner, website developer, application developer, smartphone repair, graphic designer, videographer, photographer, blogger, editor, telemarketer, event planner, life coach, personal trainer, wedding planner, party planner, interior decorator, DJ, masseuse, personal chef, food truck owner, dog walker or sitter, landscaper, handyman, caregiver, babysitter, housekeeper, class instructor for fitness, hobbies, cooking, and more.

I'm not saying formal business plans are a bad idea, but I can tell you with certainty that any effort I spent on a formal business plan with Creekmore Marketing would've been a total waste of time. I completely changed my business model after working with my first customer. No amount of planning could've prepared me for the experience that interaction taught me. I've also seen business owners waste weeks, months, even years formulating a business plan. This is an achiever mistake. The boss mantra is "action over perfection."

That being said, if you can delay action for a period of time while you save up money instead of going into debt to start your business, delay. Work your full-time job and then take on projects and build your business after hours. Your business may be a side hustle for weeks, months, or years, and there's nothing wrong with that. Trust your gut and know your profit margins so you can determine when to jump from side hustle to full-time business owner.

If you live in the United States, the SBDC (Small Business Development Center) is a phenomenal resource for new and growing businesses. It's a government-funded program that allows you to get top-notch business consulting at no cost. Visit www.whycollegeisbroken.com for more information. The SBDC helps with everything from creating a business plan, finding funding, scaling, and even selling your business. A local friend of mine spent $12,000 on a business plan prior to starting her barbecue business. This move really set her behind financially at a critical time in her business. Once she found out about the SBDC, she took the $12,000 plan there to be reworked as sales grew. She couldn't afford to work with her original consultant and in fact, needed help planning to pay off the debt she'd incurred to work with them. Today, she is debt-free and thriving, but still wishes she'd known about the SBDC sooner. There may be other programs in your state, so do your research and ask around before you pay for a consultant. And remember that business plans are optional. I'm a huge proponent of experimenting with your first customers and then developing a growth strategy.

Pro-Tip: Make your product or service subscription-based. When I first started Creekmore Marketing, I considered traveling around the country, training small business owners and their teams on how to manage their internet presence. I quickly realized most small business owners don't have the time or patience to manage their own presence. Many of them would rather pay someone to handle it for them. And get this: I could charge $500 *per month* instead of a $1000 one-time fee to train the team. Because my service was subscription-based, payday came for me whether I was working or sleeping or vacationing. Finding a way to build recurring revenue that isn't tied to your time will put you on the fast track to seven figures.

Step 2. Pick a future-proof name. I chose Creekmore Marketing, even though I'd heavily considered "Lexington Web Design and SEO." I knew the locally relevant name would resonate with people in my community, clearly communicate my services, and help with my presence on Google. Thank *God* I didn't choose that other name, because within two years, most of my business was out of state. Within three years, web design was a negligible part of my business. I've read many articles that discouraged naming your business after yourself as it could damage you and your family's reputation. But to this day, I don't regret that decision. There is something really powerful about introducing yourself with the same name as your business. Potential clients feel honored to speak to you, existing clients consider it special treatment, and disgruntled clients are immediately put at ease when you step in. Do right by your customers and this decision won't come back to bite you.

Step 3: Choose how you want to organize your business. I'd recommend meeting with a business advisor or CPA before you decide which organizational structure is best for your business. Certain structures have tax advantages, and there are different levels of liability with each.

SOLE PROPRIETORSHIP	
Ownership	One owner
Investors & Shareholders	No
Liability for debt and lawsuits	Falls on you personally, therefore people can come after your personal assets if you are sued or can't fulfill financial obligations.
Tax considerations	You pay no corporate taxes and profits are considered personal income. Profits are taxed at personal tax rate.
Other considerations	Cannot pay self W2 wages

C-CORPORATION

Ownership	One or multiple owners
Investors & Shareholders	Yes, if desired Unlimited shareholders
Liability for debt and lawsuits	Falls on the corporation (Personal assets are protected.)
Tax considerations	You pay no corporate taxes and profits are considered personal income.
Other considerations	Taxes are responsibility of the corporation. Not individually taxed.

S-CORPORATION

Ownership	One or multiple owners
Investors & Shareholders	Yes, if desired Up to 100 shareholders
Liability for debt and lawsuits	Falls on the corporation (Personal assets are protected.)
Tax considerations	Profits are only taxed on the shareholders' individual returns.
Other considerations	Required to pay reasonable W2 wages to members Must have annual meeting. Must have board of directors. Has stock. Percentage split based on stock purchased. Doesn't terminate if one member dies.

LIMITED LIABILITY COMPANY (LLC)	
Ownership	One or multiple owners
Investors & Shareholders	No
Liability for debt and lawsuits	Falls on the LLC (Personal assets are protected.)
Tax considerations	Depending on how you set up your business, you have the option to be taxed as a sole proprietorship, corporation, or partnership. Profits are taxed at personal tax rate.
Other considerations	Cannot pay self W2 wages

PARTNERSHIP	
Ownership	At least two owners
Investors & Shareholders	No
Liability for debt and lawsuits	For general partnerships, each partner is personally liable. For LLC partnerships, each partner's personal assets are protected.
Tax considerations	Profits are taxed on each partner's individual tax returns.
Other considerations	Partners are not employees and not paid W2 wages. Percentage split between partners can change anytime. Partnership immediately terminates if one dies. May take distributions but only pro rata share. No meetings required. No voting required. No company stock.

COOPERATIVE	
Ownership	All members or employees are owners
Investors & Shareholders	Yes, by default
Liability for debt and lawsuits	Liability is limited to the amount invested in the company.
Tax considerations	Profits are taxed on each member's individual tax returns.
Other considerations	

Source: http://smallbusiness.chron.com

There is another option not listed above: freelancing. Freelancing isn't a bad place to start, but your growth has a ceiling, because you're trading your time for money and you only have so much time in a day. There's a great quote from Seth Godin which says, "Freelancers get paid for their work ... Entrepreneurs use other people's money to build a business bigger than themselves so that they can get paid when they sleep."[18]

Step 4: Register for a federal tax ID number, formally known as your Employer Identification Number (or EIN). In America, you can do this at irs.gov.

Step 5: Register a trade name. This is only required if you won't be operating under your legal business name.

Step 6. Get a business license. Do a Google search for "business license in *insert your state.*" In Kentucky, for example, it's at onestop.ky.gov.

Step 7: Ask about other necessary permits or tax forms that may be required in your area. These could be federal, operational, environmental, local, or building/zoning related. In Kentucky, all of this information is available at onestop.ky.gov. Contact your local county clerk for more information.

Step 8: Set up a business bank account. You'll need your EIN, ID, and possibly other licensing. Get this set up as soon as possible so that when you cash that first check or run that first credit card, the money is deposited into your business account. This is not mandatory for sole proprietors, partnerships, or freelancers.

Step 9: Plan your exit strategy. Yes, this is something you need to think about immediately. What is your ultimate plan for your business? Do you want to be your own boss, make a good living, and run the business until you retire? Do you want to grow in hopes to one day sell for a big check? This could be accomplished by selling to another individual, as well as merging or being acquired by another firm. Do you plan to sell shares to the public in the form of an Initial Public Offering, or IPO? Do you want to scale, hire people to manage day-to-day operations, and put cash-flow on autopilot so you can make money while you sleep? This is my personal favorite.

So You're a Business Owner ... Now What?

Now it's time to get your first customer. Offer your product or service at a discount, or free, so you can get testimonials and experience under your belt. You may be tempted to choose a friend or family member, which is fine, but you'll also need to find someone you don't already know. Maybe a friend of a friend or a local business owner in your community. It's important to get out of your comfort zone and also provide your product or service to someone who will give you unbiased feedback.

With Creekmore Marketing, I developed a few case studies that proved my services helped window treatment dealers increase sales significantly. This took time, but it was well worth it.

Next, tell absolutely *everyone* what you do. A lot of new business owners hesitate to do this because they're embarrassed, or worried they'll end up embarrassed if their business doesn't take off. Be proud of yourself. You're creating something out of nothing. You don't have to be "salesy" with your friends and family. Just explain what you do, give them some business cards, and ask if they'll refer anyone they come across who's in the market for your product or service. Post on social media as well so your extended network learns about what you do.

Boss's Action Plan:

1. As you develop your vision for your business, strategize ways to stop trading your time for money so you can get paid while you sleep.

2. To be successful as a business owner, you must develop the right skill-set and mind-set. Work to improve your ability to connect with others, your attitude, your work ethic, and your accountability. Find books, podcasts, and/or videos to build these skills.

3. Determine how you will deliver more value to your customers than others in your industry. The best value propositions come from understanding your customers' pain points. What problems will you solve?

4. Consider honing in on a specific niche. Learn this industry inside and out so you can position yourself as an expert.

5. You can't be good, fast, and cheap. Pick two.

6. When you're ready, follow the nine steps to start a business:

    1. Develop a laser focused vision for your business.

    2. Pick a future-proof name.

    3. Choose how you want to organize your business.

    4. Register for a federal tax ID number.

    5. Register a trade name, if needed.

    6. Get a business license.

    7. Ask about other necessary permits or tax forms that may be required in your area.

    8. Set up a business bank account.

    9. Plan your exit strategy.

7. Get your first customer by offering your product or service at a discount, or free. Gather testimonials and create a case study.

8. Tell absolutely everyone what you do without being "sales-y."

In the next sections, we'll talk about networking and sales, which will make or break your success as an entrepreneur.

PHASE 2

Launching Your Business

Chapter 12

Elevate Your Network

*"It's not what you know, but who you know" is a
well-known saying. Yet, it is only half true. The
reality is, that in order to manage a career, grow a
business, or guide your personal or professional
endeavors, IT IS WHO KNOWS YOU!*
— Susan Roane19

I recall physically shaking as I entered my first networking event, thinking, "What the hell am I going to say?" and, "None of these people give a crap what I do." Palms profusely sweating, I shook hands with three of the twenty-five people in attendance, stuttered through my elevator pitch, then ducked out early. For weeks afterward, I was convinced networking was Satan's way of torturing those brave enough to start their own business.

I couldn't have been more wrong. Networking has taken my business from a hobby to a multi-million-dollar firm. If I had given up after my first bad experience, you wouldn't be reading this book.

If you want to take your business to the next level, you've got to have the right people know you. It's not enough to know them through the grapevine or to meet them once in passing. You need to make a lasting impression. Maybe you like talking to people; maybe you'd rather lay face-down on hot coals. Either way, I'm going to teach you how to network in a way that takes all the pressure off you and makes you stick in the minds of those you meet.

Six-Step Networking Prep:

1. <u>Take a headshot</u>. You can have it professionally taken or get a friend to take one for you. I've seen amazing headshots taken on iPhones. The key is to make sure you have plenty of natural light and that you are facing the light. (Don't take a photo where light is shining from behind you.)

2. <u>Order business cards ahead of time</u>. Your business cards should be unique. They are part of your impression. I always use my headshot on cards so people can put a face to my name. You can find fantastic templates on sites like moo.com or jukebox.com.

3. <u>Perfect your elevator pitch.</u> If you were in an elevator and someone asked you what you do, how would you respond? Develop a thirty to sixty-second elevator pitch that explains what you do, why you're passionate about your work, and why people should hire or buy from you.

4. <u>Overdress</u>. Unless the invitation specifically states the dress code is casual, I always aim to be the best dressed person in the room. I opt for a power suit or dress that makes me look like someone important. I do this even though I consider my company culture to be laid back, because it shows that I take myself, and the event, seriously. (Dressing down is a privilege that multimillionaires and billionaires earn. Ever notice how people like Mark Zuckerberg and the late Steve Jobs seem to have a closet full of T-shirts and jeans? Isn't that kind of awesome? They'd look like lazy bums if we didn't know all that they had accomplished. You're not Zuckerberg or Jobs *yet,* so keep it professional. Professional doesn't have to mean

expensive. I've purchased most of my professional wardrobe from consignment shops.)

5. Have a goal in mind. Are you searching for a mentor? A referral source? Your first customer? Get crystal clear about who you want to meet before you attend.

6. Arrive early and meet the event coordinator. I've made some killer connections by doing this that have led to keynote speaking events and long-term referral sources. These event organizers often work directly with business owners and coordinate events on a regular basis.

Have you ever heard the quote, "People don't care how much you know until they know how much you care"? It couldn't be more spot-on for networking. When you find the perfect potential mentor, client, or referral source, your goal isn't to sell them on yourself. Your goal is to show them you care. People are drawn to others who make them feel important. And isn't the end goal to make the people at the event like you and want to help you in your career?

The amazing thing is that this completely takes the pressure off you. You are *guaranteed* to keep the person you're talking to interested in the conversation by focusing it on them. You'll do this by asking lots of questions to get people talking about themselves, their career, and their dreams.

The problem is all the normal questions are *boring*. *What do you do? Where are you from?* I'm falling asleep just thinking about these conversation *snoozers*. If you want people to remember you, the key is to ask unique questions—questions that wake people up, get them thinking, and make them smile.

Here are some unique questions you can ask at your next networking event. *(You should prepare answers to these questions yourself too.)*

- "Are you introverted or extroverted? I'm trying to figure out who is loving this event and who is secretly miserable." (I say this with a teasing smile and skip this question if I'm talking to the event coordinator.)

- "What's been the highlight of your day so far?"

- "What's your story?"

- "What's your favorite part of your job?"

- "If I'm trying to refer someone to you, who would be the absolute best person I could send your way?"

- "What's your ultimate dream for your career?"

- "When you're not *insert what they do*, what do you do for fun?"

- "Do you have any kids/pets?" If they have more than one kid or pet, I always ask, "Which one is more of a handful?" I always get a chuckle and a story as a response.

- "Do you have any vacations coming up?"

Some of the above questions are my own, some are from a book called *Captivate: The Science of Succeeding with People* by Vanessa Van Edwards. The book is all about how to have dazzling conversations and build instant likeability with people you meet. It's a great read.

The Golden Rule: Avoid sales pitches at all costs. End the conversation with a question that will continue the relationship without any hint of sales intent. Here are some examples:

- Could I get your card? I'd love to pass it on to anyone in the market for "X."

- Could I get your card? I'd love to shadow you or someone at your firm for a day, if you'd be open to it. I'm really interested in your field and would love to learn more.

- Could I get your card? I'd love to pick your brain about (their industry, the business world, upcoming networking events, etc.).

- Here is my card. I'm happy to be a resource to you in any way I can.

- (Assuming you know someone else at the event.) Have you met Ted? He is an amazing graphic designer. Let me introduce you two. And before I forget, can I get your card?

There are also tons of online communities in specific industries or business niches. Don't just limit yourself to in-person networking!

To solidify the impression you made, follow up with the people you met the next morning and provide something of value. Regardless of your experience, you can be a resource to anyone. Even before I was an "expert" in my field, I found online tools that allowed me to generate twenty-page detailed reports on websites' optimization and usability. It helped business owners know why their website's performance was suffering.

Let's say I met a life insurance agent. I would send an email after the event saying, "It was great meeting you yesterday and learning more about what you do. Do you have any tips for starting the conversation about life insurance or listening for people who may be in the market? I want to keep an ear out for you so I can pass referrals your way."

A week or two later, I would follow up with an email saying, "I hope all is well. I was thinking of you the other day and wanted to send over this website report. It shares tips that should help you get more business from your website. Most of these are easy for either you or your web developer to implement. Hope it helps! Do you know of any other local networking events coming up?"

The best sales pitch is no sales pitch.

The responses to this type of email were overwhelmingly positive. Many people hired me to implement the changes. The rest were very appreciative that I would take the time to send something so valuable without expecting anything in return. It led to long-term clients, lots of referrals, invitations to leadership events, and a few local speaking gigs. I wasn't begging anyone for their business; I was baiting the hook and letting the fish come to me.

Continue nurturing the relationship by staying in touch, meeting for coffee or lunch, and passing referrals. Always ask yourself, how can I provide value to this person? Here are a few ideas:

- Ask them a question related to their industry. People love to talk about their jobs and to feel like an expert. You will learn something new at the same time!

- Use a site like SendOutCards to send a physical card in the mail from your phone for their birthday, business anniversary, a random holiday, or just to say, "Hey! Great to meet you."

- Send them something that will help their business (such as the website review I mentioned, Woorank.com).

- Follow their brand on social media and consistently comment, share, and support.

- Put them in touch with a friend who is either local or in their industry. Choose someone who would be a good referral partner. (For example, I loved it when people would introduce me to graphic designers. It was easy for me to pass them design work and for them to pass me website work.)

- Volunteer to help them with an event.

- Offer to fill in for them at BNI (BNI is a local networking group that has an attendance policy. Members *love* to have someone fill in for them when they're too busy to go. Even better, you get to meet all the people in their networking group and expand your connections).

- Pass a referral to someone. This will instantly transform your relationship from acquaintances to trusted friends.

  - Use them yourself.

  - Keep an ear out when you're with friends, family, and coworkers. Have the person's contact information on hand at all times.

  - Pay attention on social media and on sites like NextDoor. People are looking for recommendations all the time. Be ready to tag the person or put their contact information in the comments. You'll be amazed at how many referrals you can pass this way.

A quick note on finding mentors: Typically, you'll want to find someone who is succeeding at a higher level than you, both career-wise and financially. This person is valuable and he or she is likely very busy. You can still provide value to this person, but it may take some digging. Don't just ask, "What can I do for you?" Listen in conversations. Pay attention to his or her social networks and emails. Everyone has weaknesses and areas of ignorance. You may be an expert at social media campaigns where your potential mentor isn't and has been meaning to implement a marketing strategy for a long time. Maybe your potential mentor needs to hire an assistant and doesn't know how to systematize his or her tasks for someone else to take over. Identify a pain point and offer to help solve it.

I challenge you to attend two networking events in the next week. Use social media, Google, or sites like eventbrite.com and meetup.com; you'll be amazed at how many free or very inexpensive events are going on in your local community. When I started my business, I found most of my clients by joining a BNI (Business Network International) group. You can find a local chapter at https://www.bni.com.

Bottom line: Be a resource to everyone you meet without expecting anything in return. Don't ask for business or referrals. They will come to you naturally and abundantly if you add value to those around you.

Chapter 13

Mastering Sales

Hungry Salespeople Starve

Remember what I said in the last chapter about how you should never ask for referrals? That wasn't completely true. You should never ask for referrals while you're building a relationship and earning trust. Once the relationship is built on a rock-solid foundation for many months, it's okay to ask for referrals. Chances are you won't have to ask, though. You'll already be receiving them.

What do you think of when I say the word "salesperson"? For me, it was "pushy" and "pitchy" until I realized the best salespeople are neither. Dump the mental picture you have of the stereotypical "skeevy" used car salesman. We're going to be the complete opposite.

Your job as a salesperson is to know your product or service inside and out, upside down, and cut in half. Then, use that expertise to prompt the customer with questions that will cause them to sell themselves on hiring you or purchasing from you. The more you get the customer talking, the better your chances of success.

My favorite sales strategy comes from the book *SPIN Selling* by Neil Rackham[20], which was introduced to me in business school. I took a Personal Selling class that prepared me to start convincing small business owners to give me $500–$1,000 a month to market their businesses, fresh out of college. It was not easy. Most small businesses I came across had a nonexistent marketing budget, and I had to get them to invest close to their mortgage payment every month. So how did I create something out of nothing?

Before we continue, I'm going to share the exercise we completed on day one of Personal Selling. My professor took out a black ink pen, set it on a volunteer's desk, and said, "Sell me this pen."

The brave student shifted in her seat, cleared her throat, and confidently said, "This Bic 3700 is a one-of-a-kind pen. Smudge-free ink funnels through an expertly crafted ballpoint, perfect for everything from doodling to signing the dotted line. Its ergonomic shape eliminates hand cramps and can even reverse arthritis. Today only, we have a two-for-one special."

There were a few scattered claps across the room as we eagerly awaited the professor's reaction. She'd absolutely nailed it, or so we thought.

"Nope," he said, shaking his head as the once brave girl deflated in her seat. "Anyone else want to try?"

After a long, awkward silence, a guy raised his hand. His pitch was equally as creative, but ended with a confident, "How many pens would you like to buy today?"

Surely that was the error the first girl made, not asking for the sale. Right?

Wrong. The professor shook his head, took the pen, and asked for a volunteer to sit at the front of the room and be the potential customer. The professor sat in front of the student and tucked the pen in his pocket before he began speaking.

"What kind of pen do you use currently?" The professor casually said to the customer.

"An off-brand ballpoint," he responded.

"Tell me about it," he replied.

"Well, it's a blue ink pen. I got it in a pack of twenty. It's comfortable and was cheap."

"Good, I'm glad to hear that. When you're shopping for a pen, what do you look for?"

"I look for something comfortable to write with," the student said.

"Okay, sure. Does the style of the pen matter to you?"

"Not really."

"Okay. How often do you buy pens?"

"Pretty often."

"Why is that?"

"Because I lose pens all the time." He laughed.

"Don't we all," the professor chimed in with a smile. "So tell me about the most frustrating experience you've had with a pen."

"I'd say trying to find a pen when someone is telling me something important that I should be writing down." The student thought for a moment. "And when pens explode on me or in my pocket."

"Understandable. What happens when you can't find a pen and have something really important to write down?"

"I try to commit the information to memory."

"What happens if you forget the important information?"

"Well, I could miss out on an opportunity or forget to follow through on a commitment I made."

"Ah, that makes sense. What happens in your professional life when you miss opportunities or forget about commitments?"

"My career could be negatively affected. And my relationships with my coworkers may suffer."

"What about in your personal life?"

"Well, similar, it would hurt my relationships. And I could be missing out on life experiences."

The professor nodded in agreement. "So how would you feel if you knew you would always have a pen on hand that wouldn't explode or go missing?"

"I'd feel relieved," the student replied.

"Awesome. So this is a Scrivener 3.0.," he says, pulling the pen out of his pocket. "You're gonna love it. It's engineered to never explode. It has a No Leak, No Explosion guarantee or your money back. Also, it has this clamp that allows it to clip onto your pocket and stay put. No more pens MIA. Could you see yourself using this?"

"Yeah, for sure."

"Now, I have a 2.0 model, but it's cheap and you get what you pay for. It doesn't come with the warranty or the clamp. I also have an upgraded 4.0 version, but I really don't think you need that. It's more expensive because it's fashionable, but I know being flashy isn't one of your top priorities. They're normally $5 each, but we have a special going on this month. A pack of five for $15. Would you like to buy a pack today?"

"Sure would," the student said.

People buy based on emotions, not needs. If you can get your potential customer to experience the frustration of their current problem and envision the payoff of your solution in a way that evokes emotion, you've struck gold.

Your goal shouldn't be to close a sale. It should be to connect with the potential customer—to get them to open up and talk about their problems, so you can then use guided questions to get the customer to sell themselves on your product. Let the customer do the heavy lifting! Most importantly, your goal should be to make your potential customer feel important throughout the entire process—because they *are*. The SPIN strategy refers to guided questions in the following order. Note: I used my company as an example, but these questions can be applied to any product or service you want to sell.

1. **Situation**

   - What type of marketing do you currently do?

   - How long have you been doing it?

- Who are your top two to three competitors? What do you know about their marketing strategies?

2. Problem

- What problems do you have with your current marketing plan?

- Are you happy with the number of leads you're receiving from the Internet?

- What other pain points do you have in your business?

3. Implication

- In my research, I discovered that you weren't ranking very well on Google when potential customers search for your services. Do you worry you're missing out on potential business?

- You spend one to two hours per day traveling to and from jobs. Do you feel you'd be more profitable if your jobs were coming from the city you live in?

4. Need-Payoff

- How many new jobs could you handle per month? What would it mean for your bottom line if customers were finding you online and you were getting these jobs?

- Would you like to grow to the point of hiring, or increase your current staff's capacity?

- What would it mean for you if a majority of your jobs came from customers within a 10-mile radius of your store?

How to Make People Feel Important while Selling

Prepare prior to the sales call or meeting to be fully present in the conversation, enthusiastic, and patient. You may be exhausted or having a bad day, but push that aside and give the person your undivided attention. Do your research ahead of time and prepare a very detailed analysis and/or proposal presented in a professional report cover. If you are meeting the potential client at a cafe or restaurant, insist on buying and don't take no for an answer. If your schedule allows, block out two or three hours so you can talk with this potential client without checking the time. Maintain eye contact, actively listen, and always take multiple pages of notes. You may use the notes later, you may not, but regardless, it makes the person across the table feel important.

There will be days where you're exhausted and dying for a meeting or phone call to end, but your job is to never *ever* let it show.

Don't Fake It

Go a step beyond just making the person *feel* important and convince yourself this person *is* important. Mentally sell yourself on how important the person is and you will come off as very genuine, which is crucial for closing the sale. Think about how grateful you are that this person is willing to sit down and hear you out. He or she may purchase from you, which will help financially support you as you chase your dreams. This person has their own circle of influence and may be willing to spread the word about you if you go above and beyond for them. This interaction could lead to ten times the business down the road.

Have you ever heard the phrase, "She could sell ice cubes to an Eskimo?" This isn't because she's a master at sales pitches and closing the deal. It's because she genuinely connects with the people she's selling to.

Give a Crap

Be honest. Your product or service might not be for everyone. For example, our basic online marketing packages start at $595 per month. Are they for the person who just took out a $20,000 loan to start a small business and doesn't even have a single customer yet? In most cases, no.

I've had clients go out of business because they hired us and put all of their borrowed eggs into my basket. They sat back waiting for the phone to ring, when they should've kept grinding and paying down their debt. I believe in what I do, but the best smoke signals can't keep a sinking ship afloat.

As a salesperson in this situation, you may be bummed out, or even frustrated. But don't give up on this customer just because they shouldn't buy today.

When I'm talking with a potential client who isn't quite financially ready for our services, I'm honest with them. I tell them, "If it were me, I'd hold off on hiring us and hit the pavement. Join local networking and referral groups. Post on social media. Offer your product or service at a discount, or free, to get some testimonials and experience under your belt. Once you've built a solid foundation, I'll step in and help kick it into overdrive for you. In the meantime, I'm happy to be a resource to you in any way I can. If you need more hands-on help with anything like social media, I do consulting work on an hourly basis."

These people are always *so* appreciative of my advice. Over the coming weeks, they may continue to pick my brain with questions via email. They may pay for my consulting services. When cash flow is steady, I'm the first person they call. And if anyone they talk to needs marketing help, they give out my name with a glowing recommendation because they trust me completely.

Sometimes, lost sales are the best thing for your business. If you genuinely have the client's best interest at heart, business will come to you abundantly. Call it karma, the Law of Attraction, or God's grace. I have found this to be undoubtedly true.

Don't Be Afraid to Ask for the Sale

Once you're convinced the customer is sold on your product or service, ask for the sale. When selling our marketing services, I typically say, "I'm really excited to help grow your business. Would you like to get started today?"

If they say no, I don't give them some phony pitch about how we have a limited-time special if they sign up right now. While this may work on some customers, most see right through it and come away thinking you care more about your wallet and sales goals than you do about them. Oftentimes, they will say, "I need to talk to my partner about this," and I'll respond with, "I completely understand. I'd love to get on the phone with your partner and answer any questions they have. Is there a good time I could call you both next week?" Sometimes I get the follow-up appointment, sometimes they say, "Let me talk with them and get back with you."

Follow-Up for the Win

As my key salesperson Sean Larkin always says, "I follow up with all prospects until they either hire us, die, or tell me to get lost." He isn't afraid to be persistent. He doesn't go out of his way to be annoying, but he also doesn't worry about whether or not he's "bothering" the client. He invites them to our free monthly webinar or sends them ideas to improve their website. He sends seasonal cards in the mail saying things like, "I hope you're having a great summer!" He calls them to see how business is going and if they've given any further thought to bringing us on to help grow their business. According to Grant Cardone, "Eighty percent of sales are made on the fifth to twelfth contact," so persistence can really be the difference between closing a sale and letting it slip away.[21]

Know Your Profit Margins

How much profit are you actually making each time you sell a widget or service? You must know this number down to the penny. If a company has a 25 percent profit margin, they make $0.25 on every dollar of revenue earned. Visit https://www.om-nicalculator.com/business/margin to calculate your margins. What percentage do you need to make off each sale for your time invested to be worthwhile? Be prepared to adjust your pricing structure, suppliers, product, or service offerings if the numbers don't make sense. Keep in mind that this number will likely change as you grow your business. I was comfortable making $600 off a website sale when I first started my business and was doing everything myself, but as I grew and hired people, I needed to adjust my pricing to keep my profit margins healthy.

Target Monthly Income

How many sales do you need to close each month to quit your job without starving? How many sales do you need to live comfortably? How many sales to live abundantly? Run the numbers and create a target monthly income for yourself. I did this by listing my expenses into three categories:

Needs	Wants	Luxuries
Rent, electricity, water, gas, groceries, phone, medical expenses	Funds for occasional shopping, entertainment, and travel	Shopping sprees, new cars, front-row concert tickets, first-class intercontinental flights, five-star hotels

Needs	Wants	Luxuries
Enough money to make minimum debt payments.	Enough money to make two to three times your monthly debt payments	Enough money to pay 10 times your monthly debt payments, or more

If you want to quit your job, you'll have to make enough to cover your "needs" category. From there, you'll grow sales until you cover the "wants" and ultimately, the "luxuries." Wants and luxuries are different for everyone, so list things and experiences that would mean the most to you. I'd recommend factoring in an emergency fund equivalent to three to six months of income if possible. That being said, $500 is better than nothing.

Impact = Income

Your income will swell in proportion to the number of people you impact. Want to earn a million dollars? In this economy, there are so many ways to make seven figures that the only limit is your imagination. You could sell $1 pens to 1,000,000 people, sell $20 T-shirts to 50,000 people, or sell $100 online training courses to 10,000 people. For me, I sold monthly marketing packages at approximately $800 per month to just over 100 small businesses and kept these clients for a year. How many widgets, courses, packages, or services do you need to sell to hit seven figures?

Truth or Dare?

I dare you to set a quit date on your calendar and commit to quitting your job on this date. Maybe it's six months from now, nine months, or a year. Make it an aggressive but attainable goal if you hustle and hit your sales goals.

Next, I dare you to set a date on your calendar and commit to treating yourself to one thing on your luxury list. Maybe it's a shopping spree at your favorite store, backstage passes to meet your favorite band, or a trip to Europe. Maybe it's later this year, maybe it takes a couple of years to save up. The point is to put it on your calendar in stone and then adjust your actions accordingly to make it happen. Know exactly how many sales you need to make over the coming months or years to bring this dream to life.

Chapter 14

Customer Service

How are you making your customers feel? For my first few years in business, I would always leave a meeting or get off the phone thinking, "I hope I sounded good" (or knowledgeable, or professional). But really, I should've been asking myself, "How did I make that person feel?"

Things that sound good, knowledgeable, and professional can still rub people the wrong way. Since we know people will forget what we said and did, we need to focus on leaving them feeling positive and cared for.

What is the most dangerous feeling to leave a client with? It's not anger or frustration. It's the feeling that you are indifferent towards them. We know when we piss off a client and actively try to avoid that. But do you realize when a client leaves a meeting with you feeling like you don't really care?

A client should never feel like a burden or a bother, even if they are. They should never feel like you don't care, even if they drive you *crazy*. Most business owners understand this, so they develop a cheery customer service voice to flip on when they interact with customers.

The problem is, customers are more intuitive than we realize. Most can sniff out BS quickly and will pick up on phoniness either consciously or subconsciously. Think about it in your own life. When someone is being phony with you, how does it make you feel? Even if someone is being extremely nice to you, it's difficult to connect with or trust that person if you don't feel they really mean it. In fact, their efforts to be nice often have the opposite effect. You may start to dislike that person and wonder if he or she has ulterior motives.

You can't truly connect with people when you're faking it. If you force a smile while talking to a client on the phone and then roll your eyes as soon as he or she hangs up, you're faking it. I'm not saying a cheery customer service voice is a bad thing, but it needs to be backed with as much genuine positivity as you can cultivate. The key is to actualize feelings of gratitude towards your clients. I may be having a terrible day, but I take a minute or two before I hop on the phone with a client to remind myself how appreciative I am for their business. Each client I have allows my business to grow, which creates more income and opportunities for growth for every employee. This puts me in the right mind-set to connect with the client by showing authentic enthusiasm and interest, as well as providing compliments that are sincere and specific.

Don't go into autopilot mode. Have you ever had a conversation where your brain was in autopilot mode and you weren't really paying close attention? This happens when we small talk. Where are you from? What do you do? Again, these are conversation snoozers that leave both parties feeling bored and disengaged. Refer back to the unique set of questions from chapter 12 on elevating your network. Ask questions that snap your customers out of auto-pilot mode and get them thinking. This will show them you genuinely care about getting to know them and will leave a lasting impression.

Honesty is always the best policy. When my grandmother passed away, I was open with my clients about it because I knew I may seem a little less cheery than normal. I didn't want them picking up on this vibe and taking it personally. My honesty allowed me to connect with my clients through shared sympathy and gave me a very valid excuse for not being my normal peppy self.

Is your customer being fake with you? When you're engaged in the conversation, you can use intuition to gauge the customer's emotional state and get them to open up to you. Customers aren't always honest and sometimes hide their real feelings in an effort to be professional and to avoid confrontation. Learn when to ask feedback questions throughout the conversation, such as, "What are your thoughts?" or "How do you feel about this?" or "What do you think?" This is a great way to get clients to open up to you, as long as you don't overuse it. Ask feedback questions too often and you may come across as unsure or insecure.

Create an environment where honest feedback is encouraged. When we reveal a new website design to a client, our primary goal is to get honest feedback from them. We say, "Here is your website. Now, you aren't hurting my feelings if you don't like something. Please be brutally honest with me. I want you to absolutely love this website and will keep tweaking it until you do. How do you feel about it?" I can see something flicker in their eyes, as they realize: *Oh, I can be real with this person. I don't have to sugarcoat my response.*

To respect the client's time and personality, gauge how they would like the conversation to go before it begins. When reviewing monthly marketing reports with our clients, I always ask at the beginning of the call, "Would you like a deep-dive review of this report, or a high-level overview of the key performance indicators (KPIs)?" and also, "How much do you know about these reports? I don't want to overexplain or underexplain." Overexplaining is a common rookie mistake for people who are new to customer service roles. They try to fill the empty space in the conversation with knowledge and facts in an effort to inform and show competence. Some customers love to hear all the nitty-gritty details; others couldn't care less and will end up bored or annoyed if you give long, detailed explanations. Ask questions to gauge the situation up front so you can cater your delivery according to their personality and time frame. This is a hugely valuable skill that isn't taught in school and will give you a leg up on your competitors.

Trust your gut. If you get the impression the customer is "off" during the conversation, they either have an issue with your service or an unrelated issue. Without prying, I will make it a point to ask questions like, "How has business been lately?" "What else is going on in your life right now?" or "Is anything frustrating you right now that I can help with?" Because my clients sense I'm being genuine, they typically open up to me.

Don't second-guess yourself during a customer service interaction. Assume everyone likes you and thinks you are extremely competent. Doing this has been a total gamechanger for me. Now, I'm not naïve. I know this isn't always true, but I always give my customers the benefit of the doubt because insecurity can be felt in person or over the phone. If I second-guess whether or not someone likes me, I'm thinking too much about myself and not enough about them. I'm more scatterbrained and less confident. I tend to make more mistakes in this state of mind, so assuming everyone likes me and thinks I am competent gives me the confidence to act more likeable and competent. It's a self-fulfilling prophecy.

On the flip side, if you hold the belief that someone doesn't like you, you will subconsciously act more standoffish towards them. This vibe *kills* your ability to connect with people. I wonder how many potential relationships, friendships, and business partnerships die because one person is worried that the other person doesn't like them, so they act nervous and standoffish, and therefore, it becomes true— the other person doesn't like them. Assuming the other person likes you puts you in the right mind-set to connect with *anyone*. (If they don't actually like you,

I'd bet that'll change the more you interact with them warmly and confidently. If not, that's their problem.)

Do you know the phrase, "Kill them with kindness"? It's a double-edged sword. If a client is upset, killing them with *genuine* kindness is a very effective customer service strategy. Killing clients with *fake* kindness is the surest way to send the relationship up in flames. Again, clients will pick up on any phoniness or snarky undertones in your voice. They will either get more angry, or simply disconnect with you completely.

When a customer is upset, they want to know you care, you will fix it, and it won't happen again. If you immediately take personal responsibility and apologize, even if it wasn't your fault, you will win. Here is our protocol at Creekmore Marketing when a problem arises:

- Call the client immediately and apologize.

- Fix it right away.

- Make up for it, if appropriate.

- Share a plan for preventing it from ever happening again.

- If the client played a role in this issue occurring, gently tell them how they can help you help them.

- Always check in a week or two later to make sure they are happy.

I'll share two examples. We were managing social media for one of our clients and accidentally posted the wrong website link on her Facebook page. We had posted another client's website link, which she was very upset about. I called immediately to apologize and let her know how horrified I was. I could tell she had planned to give me a piece of her mind, but was surprised to hear I was just as upset as she was. Remember this: It's nearly impossible to argue with someone when they are agreeing with you. If a client is upset, I always look at it from their perspective and aim to agree with them, instead of defend myself or make excuses. I said, "I'm embarrassed. This is completely unacceptable and I'm very sorry. I'm having a meeting with the social media manager who posted this as soon as we get off the phone to make sure this never happens again. She is normally very on the ball, so I'm confident that it won't. I'll make sure you get three extra social media posts to make up for it. How does that sound?" The funny thing is problems like this can actually deepen your relationship with clients. It's ironic, but we now have a better relationship with this client than we did before the social media mistake because the way we handled it built trust.

Now, here's an example where the client got upset about something that was his fault. I had a client call on the verge of screaming because he was confused about his reports. He thought his number of clicks on an ad was his ranking on Google. We thought he would be thrilled to see 91 clicks on a certain keyword, but he completely lost it because he assumed that meant he was ranking 91 pages back on Google. My first response was, "Oh no. Let me pull up the report right now so we can get to the bottom of this," which showed him I took the problem seriously. Once I identified the issue, I said, "I think you're going to be relieved when you hear this. I should've gotten you on the phone before I sent these, because I see the report itself isn't as clear as it should be. It's trying to explain that you received 91 clicks on this keyword from your ads. It doesn't mean you are ranking 91 pages back on Google. Do you see what I'm talking about? I'm sorry for the confusion. I'm actually really happy with this number!"

Here the client was completely in the wrong, but I still found a way to accept responsibility and apologize for the role I played. He ended up feeling silly and apologizing to me.

This may be an unpopular opinion, and maybe it's the southerner in me, but I always tell myself, "I have no shortage of apologies." I could say "I'm sorry" 1000 times without taking a hit to my pride or confidence. This makes me *unstoppable* when it comes to customer service. While your competitors are busy tripping over their egos, you can apologize, keep your customer relationships solid, and keep the cash flowing in.

Now, actualizing feelings of gratitude will only get you so far. Don't be afraid to cut ties with clients who drain your energy and don't serve your bigger vision. We'll discuss this further in chapter 16 on setting boundaries and firing clients.

Lastly, always follow through on your word. If you tell a client you are going to do something, do it. If you tell them you will call them at a certain time, or arrive at a certain time, make it happen. If your client finds you unreliable, it'll be difficult to regain their trust and confidence again. When I interact with a customer over the phone or in person, I take detailed notes and follow up the same day on all items discussed. Things rarely slip through the cracks, but if they do, I take personal responsibility, apologize, make it right, and assure them it won't happen again.

In summary, be intuitive, genuine, and proactive with your customer service. You will wow your customers and make your competitors look like rookies.

The better your customer service, the more repeat and referral business you will get. In the next chapter, we'll discuss how to master your time to maximize your productivity and income.

Chapter 15

Master Your Time

You didn't quit the 9-to-5 to work 24/7.

Dealing with stress has been the biggest challenge I've faced in my entrepreneurial journey. We live in a workaholic culture where stress and busyness are the standard and working long hours is praised. As my business grew, so did my priority list. It quickly became unmanageable, so what did I do? I worked more. Late nights, pumping myself full of caffeine, trying to work through a list of tasks and projects that seemed never-ending became the norm.

Busyness is addicting. Over time, even when I managed to finish my list of tasks, I'd look for other things to do. I'd think to myself, *Maybe I can work ahead so I don't have to pull all-nighters anymore.* The funny thing was, I didn't have to pull all-nighters at all. I needed to learn to master my time.

Workaholics are revered in American culture, but don't be fooled. These aren't professional superheroes. Most of the time, workaholics are overwhelmed people with ineffective time management skills.

For years, I was constantly telling the people around me, through exasperated sighs, *"I'm so busy,"* or *"I just can't seem to catch up."* Looking back, part of me felt proud to be so busy and part of me was crying for help. I wasn't taking ownership of my situation. Now, when I feel like complaining about my workload, I tell myself, "Yeah, you're so busy. So what are you going to *do* about it?"

In the following sections, I will share exactly, step-by-step what I did about it. You've got big dreams and you're going to have to take major action to achieve them. Your schedule and task lists are going to fill up quicker than you think. Want to jump from five figures to six figures and ultimately seven figures? It all boils down to mastering and maximizing your time.

I recently vowed to myself to never complain about being "so busy" to anyone for three reasons. One, I am extremely grateful for my prosperous business. Two, effective leaders don't complain. They problem solve. Three, I am capable of building systems and processes that will reduce my workload and free my time. You are too, and in this chapter I'm going to show you how.

GET RELIGIOUS WITH ORGANIZATION

I'm a messy person by nature. I've always thought of myself as someone who could find order in chaos, so why waste time organizing? This anti-system was a perfect system when I had ten clients, but when I reached thirty, forty, *fifty*, I was forgetting client names, overlooking emails, and missing deadlines. So, I buckled down and started using a Customer Relationship Management (CRM) system and Project Management tool.

These tools are crucial if you want to stay sane and scale your business. A CRM tool manages your client communications and important information. Today, everything we know about our clients goes in our CRM tool. Contact information, contracts, payment dates, key contacts, etc. Our CRM keeps a log of every email we send categorized by company and contact. We also jot down notes after every phone call we have. When a client calls out of the blue, I don't have to rack my brain to remember what we talked about last month. And if you have a team, you'll want to know who talked to what client last and about what. Keeping your CRM tool up to date must be a non-negotiable daily habit for you and for everyone on your team.

We use Basecamp to manage projects, priority lists, and tasks. It ensures deadlines are never missed and things never slip through the cracks. I recommend it for both individuals and teams. We have a separate "Basecamp," or project, for each client. A client sends us pictures? They're stored in their Basecamp under Docs and Files. A client wants us to add a promotion to their website starting April 15th? An assignment is created, delegated to the appropriate person, and set with a due date of April 14th so we can ensure it goes live the morning of the 15th.

BRAIN DUMP

To master your time, you must take everything floating around in your head—every single thing—and write it down. Do this before you start your work for the day, whether it be first thing in the morning or the night before. I have an online priority list through Basecamp where I brain dump everything I have to do or am thinking about into one list.

Do not skip this step. It's the foundation of time mastering, but it also eases that scatter-brained, holy-crap-I-have-so-much-to-do-where-do-I-start feeling. Write down every task, errand, project, person you need to call back and idea floating around in your head. From here, you can prioritize, dispose, automate, delegate, and *slay*.

PRIORITIZING

Prioritizing your brain dump is the next step. (Prioritizing itself should *always* be your first daily priority, at the top of your list.) Tackling your to-dos before prioritizing is a surefire way to make sure you stay stressed and ineffective.

Look at your brain dump and ask yourself, "If I could only get *one* thing on this list complete before I leave today, what would be most important?" Then restructure your priority list until the most important items are at the top and the least important at the bottom.

If you're dreading a particular task, like dealing with a project that's blown up or calling a particular client, move this to the top of your list. Most people do the opposite. They'll push off the things they're dreading because they don't want to deal with them. Knocking it out right off the bat allows you to move past the problem, instead of worrying about it throughout the day. Try this for a week; I guarantee you'll feel happier, less stressed, and more productive.

DISPOSING

Success is not about adding, it's about taking away. The 80/20 rule, also known as the Pareto Principle, is a great way to think about this. Originally used as a way for economists to explain why 20 percent of Italy's population seemed to hold 80 percent of the country's wealth, the Pareto Principle is essentially a way to understand why a "minority of inputs results in a majority of outputs."[23] What does this have to do with mastering your time? Well, have you ever heard the phrase "work smarter, not harder?" This is essentially the Pareto Principle in a nutshell when applied to time management: according to the Pareto Principle, 20 percent of your work will lead to 80 percent of your results, so learn where to best apply your efforts. Successful people know this and leverage it.

Is everything in your prioritized list absolutely crucial? As your business grows, you must say no to anything that isn't an income-producing or goal-oriented activity. For example, after I launched a website for a client, he called and asked for help setting up email on his computer. I said, "Sure, the setup should be fairly easy." Turns out, his computer had a virus, and with his lack of technical savvy, the call took nearly two hours. He was unwilling to pay for my time. After all, I told him it would be easy!

I should have said no off the bat and recommended he find a local IT company to help. Email setup is *not* part of my vision for my company. I could've spent those two hours prospecting a new client or knocking out other important tasks on my priority list.

Get crystal clear about your vision for your company, as well as your product and service lines. Dispose of every task that doesn't fall in line with that vision. Be vicious about it. Everything you say no to allows you to say yes to something else, something more important to your vision, something income-producing. Steve Jobs famously said at Apple's 1997 World Wide Developers Conference, "Focusing is about saying no." He later said, "I'm as proud of many of the things we haven't done as the things we have done. Innovation is saying no to a thousand things."[24]

There is a phenomenal book called *The ONE Thing* by Gary W. Keller and Jay Papasan[25]. It's a simplified version of the 80/20 rule that centers around asking yourself, "What's the ONE thing I can do, such that by doing it everything else will become easier or unnecessary?"

Oftentimes, this ONE thing is building a system—a system for automating or delegating which will multiply your time in the long run.

AUTOMATING

> "Automation is to your time exactly what compounding interest is to your money." – Rory Vaden, Author and Speaker at TEDxDouglasville[26].

Next, determine what you can put on autopilot. You'll be shocked at how many tasks can be automated in today's world. Paying your bills, invoicing clients, emailing prospects, your sales funnel, scheduling appointments, bookkeeping, gathering testimonials, asking customers for referrals, answering your phone, posting on social media, the list goes on and on. I've created a list of automation tools and platforms you can find in the

Resources section of this book or online at www.whycol-legeisbroken.com.

Invest time in setting up automated systems. It may take you an extra hour or two today, but how much time will it save you over a month? Six months? A year?

I'd highly recommend watching Rory Vaden's TED talk on "How to Multiply Your Time" and reading his book *Procrastinate on Purpose*. His principles inspired my approach to time mastering.

DELEGATING

> *"Deciding what not to do is as important as*
> *deciding what to do." — Steve Jobs*[27]

What on your list could feasibly be delegated to someone else or outsourced? Determine which items on your list could be handled by someone else without the universe exploding. (In chapter 18, I'll explain how to hire help inexpensively or for free, so don't worry about money for now.) Can an assistant handle your emails? Can an answering-service take your phone calls? Can you hire an unpaid or minimum-wage intern to handle data entry, organization projects, networking, identifying prospective clients, updating your website, or posting on social media?

If someone can do a task 80 percent as good as you, delegate it. I know it's scary to hand the reins over, but remember that you're not aiming for perfection here. You're aiming to get rich, grow a business, and build your legacy. Whoever takes over may make mistakes here and there, but don't sweat the small stuff. Every time I was afraid to delegate, I would find within a day or two that while some areas of the task didn't have my "personal touch," others were being done better without my having to invest time, brainpower, or willpower.

Is there a particular task you absolutely dread doing? Find a way to delegate it. You didn't become your own boss to do stuff you hate.

Finally, delegate anything you suck at. Settlers try to ignore their weaknesses. Achievers try to improve their weaknesses. Bosses delegate their weaknesses and focus on their strengths. That's where the money is.

Did You Know Delegating Doesn't Just Have to Apply to Your Work Life?

As my business grew and I'd paid off all debt aside from my mortgage, I hired a maid, lawn care crew, and a personal assistant to handle things like errands, grocery shopping, and walking the dogs. Do you know how nice it was to get off work and actually be able to relax in a clean home with a mowed lawn and stocked fridge? It's *so* much cheaper than you realize to outsource your personal life. The maid, for example, I hired through Care.com; the cost was less than $100 per month to clean our house every two weeks for three hours at $15 per hour. While some may consider this a wasteful expense, it was easy for me to justify. In college, I was spending $100 *every week* eating out and going to bars. What wasteful expenses can you cut to hire help and improve your lifestyle?

WHAT TO KEEP

Short-term, you'll have to keep certain things on your list until you can come up with a system to automate or delegate. You're going to block out time to build one system or process per day — a written, step-by-step how-to guide. That way, you'll only have to train someone once on how to do it and they will always have a reference. It may require you to put in extra hours upfront, but I promise you this time invested will pay off tenfold.

Long-term, plan to fill your priority list with two things: projects you love and excel at, and income-producing activities — actions that generate leads and sales. Hopefully, these are one and the same or can eventually become one and the same.

Look at your prioritized list. Chances are, only 20 percent of your daily actions (or maybe even less) are actually growing your bank account. Examples of non-income producing activities are reading books, watching webinars, attending training sessions, blogging, and doing industry research on social media. Don't get me wrong; these tasks are important, but if you focus too much energy on them without actual prospecting, you'll find yourself with a hobby, not a business.

SCHEDULING OUT

What is most important overall may not be most important to complete today. For example, you may have a huge design project you're working on for your biggest client that is due in a week. It's easily your top priority, as it's going to generate the most income. However, you stroll into the office and find voicemail from two smaller clients. One is concerned that business is slow and is unhappy with website performance. The other noticed an error on their website that they'd like to have fixed ASAP. Oh, and on top of that, you've got eighty-seven unread emails, some of which you can tell at first glance look important.

You may feel inclined to focus on the big project. You're making way more money on it, plus, let's face it, you're dreading dealing with your unhappy clients and all those emails. But if you don't return the calls and time sensitive emails, your clients feel ignored. They go from upset to angry and start complaining about your service to fellow business owners or online. At the end of the day, you have a damaged reputation; but hey, you've made some headway on your big project.

Instead, push off the design project, even if these unexpected client issues take up a huge chunk of your day. Then, with whatever time is left, ask yourself, "What's the ONE thing I can do that will make my unresolved tasks easier or unnecessary?"

In this case, the answer may be to hire help. So instead of working on your big project, spend the rest of the day setting up ads for an assistant or Client Relations Manager.

So technically, at the end of the day, you've accomplished nothing that was originally on your priority list, but it's not the end of the world because you still have six days before your design project is due. Rory Vaden calls this "procrastinating on purpose."

Most people keep one to-do list. Every time a priority arises, they add it to the list. When starting or growing a business, keeping one list is a guaranteed way to feel stressed out. There are *so* many things to do and new priorities will always arise. For me, my priority list was so long, I dreaded even looking at it.

Then I learned the magic of scheduling out my priorities. I now create fourteen priority lists at a time (creating daily to-do lists two weeks in advance), each labeled by date. (I do this online, through Basecamp in the "Messages" section.) Look at your to-do list and ask, "Which tasks can be tackled on another day?" or "What is the latest date this task needs to be completed by?" Then, move that task to another day and forget about it. Don't let it stress you out or take up an ounce of your brainpower.

SETTING MEETINGS WITH YOURSELF

"The key is not to prioritize what's on your schedule, but to schedule your priorities."

- Stephen Covey, author of The Seven Habits of Highly Effective People[28]

To make sure you actually tackle the tasks or projects you schedule out in advance, you must set distraction-free meetings with yourself. At least half of my workweek schedule is blocked out for meetings I set with myself. I block the time off in my calendar, put my phone on silent, don't check any notifications, and get to work on my most important tasks.

Before I did this, a client or colleague would ask, "Can we meet on Monday at nine a.m.?" I'd look at my calendar and say, "Sure! I'm wide open." Then I would have to work late nights to catch up from all my meetings and calls. I was spinning in circles and could not figure out why I wasn't catching up.

Now, because I set meetings with myself to tackle important projects, I never have to work past five p.m. if I don't want to.

BREAKING THE BUSYNESS ADDICTION

As I said before, busyness is addicting and entrepreneurs crave accomplishment, which makes us prone to workaholism and perpetual stress. In our society, the norm is trading health for wealth throughout our working years until we're old and sick, when we'll pay *any* amount of money to feel better. Ironic, isn't it? What's the point of being a millionaire if you don't feel good enough to enjoy the lifestyle wealth can bring you?

Health is a *competitive advantage* in today's business world. I prioritize health because it makes me feel good, gives me energy to kick ass and outperform my competition, and provides me the energy to enjoy my hard-earned money. We'll dive deeper into health in chapter 23.

We all know overworking can be physically and emotionally draining, but did you know it can drain your bank account too?

It's true. For years, I tried to wear too many hats; I juggled leading my team, emails, bookkeeping, customer service, marketing, sales, and office administration. My husband would ask,

"How long until you burn out again?" It eventually got to the point where once every month or two, I'd be so emotionally drained, I'd be ready to throw in the towel.

When I finally got serious about mastering my time by discarding, automating, delegating, and breaking my addiction to busyness, something amazing happened. Not only could I finally relax and enjoy my nights and weekends, but my income started to grow because I was focusing on money-making activities. I spent most of my day filming marketing videos, networking, prospecting new clients, or closing a sale. I was enjoying life more, making more money, and was less busy than I'd ever been.

STARVING DISTRACTION

Just as busyness can be addicting, so can distraction. Distraction is a temporary break from the pressures of the workday. When we are overwhelmed, we actively seek distraction. Laughing at a funny meme your friend tagged you in releases endorphins that biologically cause you to crave more distractions.

But every minute you spend distracted is another minute you'll have to spend making up for that distraction. I don't know about you, but I'd rather spend those minutes away from my desk, relaxing, traveling, going on adventures with my loved ones, or maybe just taking a nap. At first, my "distraction starving" drove the people around me crazy. I was always hearing, "You never answer my texts!" I got used to explaining, "I don't check texts during work hours. It keeps me focused and allows me to get off earlier and spend more time with my friends and family."

So, at this point, your daily priority list and schedule should align with your vision for your company. Now, it's time to get in the zone.

What Is Getting in the Zone?

Blocking out sixty- or ninety-minute periods to starve all distractions and be productive.

How Do You Get in the Zone?

I turn my phone on do-not-disturb mode, so that calls, texts, emails, and social media notifications don't derail my productivity. I refuse to think or stress about anything else going on in my workday. I sell myself on why the task at hand is important and what the payoff will be. "If I invest an hour into automating our client's recurring monthly payments, I will save four hours per month or two days per year. I could take off every Friday an hour early, or spend two extra days off traveling the world with my family."

I recommend coming up with a daily routine that starves distraction.

- **Develop a Morning Routine.** For me, it's eating a healthy breakfast and getting a bit of light exercise in the morning, typically a fifteen-minute walk while listening to a business book or inspirational podcast. Sometimes it includes meditating or tidying up. While writing this book, my morning always included getting at least 500 words written per day before I started work-related tasks.

- **Review Today's Priority List and Re-prioritize If Necessary.** Make sure your day is scheduled around income-producing and/or time-freeing activities. Go through the process of prioritizing, discarding, automating, delegating, deciding what to keep, scheduling out, and setting meetings with yourself. The tasks that remain on today's list should be feasible to accomplish or start today. I make sure I have at least one sixty-minute block of time to create an automation or delegation process that will save me time down the road, even if it means temporarily pushing off something that feels more important. The task I'm dreading most goes at the top of my list to be tackled first.

- **Visualizing.** Visualization can be a powerful mental tactic to make accomplishing tasks easier. When you dread doing something, you subconsciously make it seem much more difficult and time-consuming in your mind. Visualizing the step-by-step process in vivid detail helps you realize the task isn't such a monster and makes it easier to get started.

  For example, I pushed off transitioning to Quickbooks for months in the early years of my business because it felt like such an overwhelming project. We used a simple, but limited, automated bookkeeping software that didn't allow me to pull a profit and loss statement, which was a problem. When I finally gathered the motivation to start the transition, I did it by visualizing the process. I told myself, "I'm going to move over our recurring invoices first and knock out ten invoices per day. I'll log into Quickbooks, pull up our current bookkeeping software, click the big gray pause button recurring invoice on our current system. Then, I'll click the big green "Create New" button in Quickbooks and import the data. I'll schedule the invoice to send on a recurring basis and voila! Each one will take me 5 minutes or less."

- **Protect Your Time**. To do this, you must be aware of time-wasters at work and avoid them at all costs. The most common time-wasters are distractions, interruptions, task-switching or multitasking, gossiping, meetings that are unnecessarily long or unnecessary in the first place, short gaps between meetings, and disorganization.

Are *you* wasting time? Tom Kite said, "You can always find a distraction if you're looking for one."[29] Sometimes it's not your talkative coworker you need to worry about; it's you. Again, we seek distraction when we are overwhelmed, so if you need to go back to your prioritizing exercises to get clear about what is most important to focus on now, do it. Self-awareness is key for mastering your time. That being said, you may also need to set boundaries with your coworkers. At Creekmore Marketing, we often tell each other, "I'm going into focus mode," then pop in our headphones or shut the door. We've made it a priority to minimize distractions and only interrupt someone in focus mode if it's a true emergency.

Let's dive deep into each of these time-wasters so you can understand them better and avoid them like the plague.

- **Self-interruptions.** Most of us self-interrupt more often than we are actually interrupted. Example: You're compiling a report and suddenly remember an upcoming trip you need to book a flight for, so you check Expedia for airfare. According to research conducted by the University of California, each interruption costs you an average of 23 minutes and 15 seconds to get back on task[30]. Some interruptions are quick: "Sign this paper" or "Are you free for a call next Tuesday?" Others require you to switch mental gears completely and engage in another task or conversation.

- **Multi-tasking.**

  "He who chases two rabbits, catches neither."
  — Anonymous

  According to the Harvard Business Review, multitasking can lead to a 40 percent decrease in productivity.[31] Whether you are trying to do two things at once, switching back and forth between two tasks, or working on a task while simultaneously thinking about another.

- **Gossiping.** Not only is gossiping an obvious time waster, but it can seriously damage your culture and relationships at work. As a leader, I respect people who avoid talking badly about others behind their back. If you have a problem with someone, go to them and talk it out. If you're not going to do that, mind your own business.

- **Unnecessarily long meetings.** Have you ever been to an hour-long meeting where you spent 15 minutes on small talk, 10 minutes compiling materials, 15 minutes talking about the problem, and 20 minutes chatting about something completely off-topic? According to an article in The Huffington Post, simple tricks like setting a strict time limit for meetings, having a clear purpose for each meeting, and ensuring that only team members who are directly involved with the issue at hand are present can help you cut down on meeting times.[32]

- **Unnecessary meetings.** If a meeting can be avoided altogether by sending a group email, send the email.

- **Time between meetings.** Do you ever *really* accomplish anything in those random fifteen- or thirty-minute periods between meetings? While breaks are healthy, too many staggered meetings can suck up so much time you could spend being productive. I aim to schedule my meetings back to back whenever possible.

- **Disorganization.** According to Rory Vaden, the average person spends an hour per day looking *for stuff.*[33] That's almost fifteen days per year we spend looking for things! What a waste of our lives. Get organized to minimize the amount of time it takes you to find things, during and outside of work.

- **Schedule Out Actively throughout the Day.** I told you to schedule out anything that can be tackled on another day. As you go about a normal workday, things will pop up. Responsibilities will fall on your plate. Sometimes you will need to reorganize today's priority list to fit them in. Many times you'll need to add tasks to your to-do list for tomorrow or next Monday or the end of the month. Schedule it out and forget about it until you have the time to give it the attention it deserves.

- **Leverage Willpower.** Willpower by definition is the control exerted to do something or restrain impulses. Imagine you have a tank of willpower that slowly depletes throughout the day as you restrain distraction, impulses, and exert control to stay focused and get things done. People who have mastered their time understand and leverage this concept by tackling their most difficult tasks when their willpower is at its highest—first thing in the morning. Don't wait until the end of the day to make the dreaded phone call or deal with that project that's blowing up. If you do this, you'll stress throughout the day and ultimately have to deal with the problem when your energy is at its lowest, which leads to burnout and bad decisions. Be honest with yourself: What are you dreading doing most right now? Add it to the top of your list for tomorrow morning and knock it out.

- **Refuse to Participate in Stress**. In our society, it's common to hear people say, "Man, I'm so stressed out." But bosses realize that stress is a choice. 0You can choose not to participate in stress or worry. Stressing and worrying cannot change your situation; it can only make you feel bad and discourage you from taking action. Action is the only thing that can actually change your situation. You may think someone who isn't concerned about a serious problem doesn't understand the gravity of that problem, but in fact, maybe they just understand that worrying is counter-productive. (Now, I realize for people with anxiety disorders, choosing not to participate in stress can be impossible at times. While these tips may help, squelching stress may require more effort, coupled with therapeutic or medicinal remedies.) If you master your time with the above principles, most of your workday stresses will eliminate themselves. However, here are a few additional steps you can take to minimize stress:

- **If you get overwhelmed throughout the day,** *take breaks.* You should be getting up to move around: take a walk and get your blood pumping at least every two hours. Do not make the mistake of sitting for eight hours straight and then wondering why you feel so tired and stressed out all the time.

- **Visualize the Worst Case Scenario**. Strangely enough, this is an extremely effective strategy for keeping your worries in perspective. Think about that project or situation you're stressed about. Now imagine the worst possible scenario that could come from it. A client hates your new designs and curses you out. They demand a refund. You begrudgingly give them the money back, feeling totally bummed out and pissed off. You take a financial hit, as well as a hit to your confidence. Not a good week. But is it the end of the world? No. There will be other clients who love your designs and treat you with respect. Time will pass. It may take a week, or a month, or half a year, but eventually, this won't matter anymore. You won't even think about it. So is it really worth losing sleep over? On top of that, if you weren't so busy worrying, you could have spent time revamping your design or maybe fired your jerk of a client before things blew up in your face. I've found that rarely, if ever, does my worst-case scenario happen.

- **Deep Breathing/Meditating** When you breathe deeply, your brain sends signals to your body to de-stress and relax. I remember reading about this and then trying one or two breaths during a really stressful time and then thinking, *"Deep breathing doesn't do anything."* Turns out, I wasn't giving it enough time or effort because I didn't believe it would work. And as we discussed before, whether you think you can or you think you can't, you're right. I personally like to combine deep breathing with taking a quick walk. I return feeling calm and clear-headed.

Many people combine deep breathing with meditation or yoga. Both of these practices involve you giving yourself permission to ignore everything going on in your life and clear your mind. We think thousands of thoughts per day. Clearing your mind of this constant mental ping-pong can be challenging, but so rewarding to your health and stress levels. Mantras are words or phrases used to assist in concentration during yoga. My favorite mantra is "bliss." Sometimes when I need inspiration to write, I'll use mantras like, "Creativity pours out of me effortlessly." You can choose any word or phrase you'd like, as long as it is anything that makes you happy, calms you down, or propels you towards a goal you'd like to accomplish.

If you choose to meditate, aim to make it a daily practice. Pick the same time and place each day, a designated space that is quiet and calming to you. At first, you may choose to use a guided meditation app such as Calm or Headspace. Set aside five or ten minutes to breathe deeply, clear the mind, and focus on an empowering mantra.

Be patient with yourself. You aren't doing it wrong if your mind drifts back into thought. Simply bring your mind back to your mantra without judgment and continue breathing deeply. If you find yourself wondering if you are doing it right, tell yourself, "Yes. I'm doing great."

Boss's Action Plan:

1. **Get organized.** Color code, label, and create systems for *everything*. Create to-do lists for at least a week into the future.

2. **Brain dump.** Write down everything you have to do, every client you have to call, every event you want to attend, every deadline you need to hit onto one list.

3. **Dispose.** What can you say no to? Focus on saying yes to income-producing activities, instead.

4. **Automate and delegate.** What can you put on autopilot? What can you delegate to others? Invest the time now to

set up automation systems and delegation processes so you can save time later.

5. **Schedule out**. What must be completed today? What can be pushed off to another day? Move any non-pressing tasks to future to-do lists so they don't take up an ounce of today's brainpower.

6. **Schedule meetings with yourself**. Do not make the mistake of leaving your schedule open. Block out time to work on your to-do list and tackle major projects. Don't forget to factor in time to deal with unexpected calls and emails.

7. **Starve distraction**. Go into focus mode on a regular basis and don't let anything that isn't a true emergency interrupt you.

8. **Refuse to participate in stress**. Tackle the tough projects first. Take breaks. Go for a walk. Meditate.

Chapter 16

Setting Boundaries and Firing Clients

Everyone in the business world deals with headache clients, those whose name on the caller ID makes you cringe, those who don't respect your time or boundaries, who call at nine p.m. and expect you to answer. You give them the moon and the stars, and they're mad you didn't include a *planet*.

If you haven't had the pleasure of dealing with someone like this, trust me, you will at some point in your career. People like this expect you to be at their beck and call whenever they please because *they are the customer*. They feel entitled to call you after-hours, show up without an appointment, repeatedly text, email, and call until you respond; the list goes on and on. They demand respect from you without showing respect in return.

Paradoxically, difficult clients who suck up most of your attention are the ones you should give the *least* attention. Clients like this are toxic to your health, happiness, and business. They stress you out, keep you up at night, and drain your energy—*energy you could be using to make money* by pampering your existing client base or bringing in new clients.

It's important to set firm boundaries early on, and if the client doesn't abide by them, swiftly part ways.

Looking back, the most stressful times in my business were the times I tried to please people who couldn't be pleased. These are the clients you will learn to fire with a smile on your face. There are, however, many clients out there who would shape up if you set some ground rules. I'll share a couple of scenarios and how to set boundaries in each.

#1. While you were in a meeting, a borderline headache client called and left three voicemails.

You didn't answer the first two times, so naturally, they thought they'd try you a third.

Solution: Call back and ask what the emergency is. (Unless it was an actual emergency, which it rarely is, the client will be caught off-guard by this question and hopefully understand they went overboard on the calls.) Explain that out of respect, you don't answer calls when in meetings with other clients (just as you wouldn't answer a call if you were in a meeting with them). Lastly, assure the person that if you miss their call in the future, you will return it as soon as your schedule allows.

#2. A client refuses to schedule calls/meetings with you in advance.

They'd rather call you out of the blue whenever they feel like it.

In the early stages of your business, this isn't a problem. You're probably thinking, "Please, blow up my phone; I'm just happy to have a client."

This becomes a problem as your business grows. As you book up with meetings and calls, you'll start to plan your days in advance. This is where it's crucial to sharpen your time-management skills, mainly by prioritizing, setting meetings with yourself, building systems, staying organized, breaking the busyness addiction, and blocking distractions (see chapter 15 if you need a refresher).

The week prior to writing this, I stepped out of a meeting with a triple whammy—voicemail, text, *and* email from a client saying, "Please call me." I'd asked this client on multiple occasions to schedule meetings with me in advance; she said that was too difficult for her schedule and she wanted to make herself available for her customers. For me, to achieve maximum productivity, I regularly book myself solid with client or team meetings, phone calls, and most importantly, meetings I set with myself to tackle important projects. I simply don't have time or patience to take phone calls out of the blue on someone else's agenda.

This is the email I sent her at the end of the day:

"I am very busy and most clients are booking meetings with me two to three days in advance. I know it's difficult for you to schedule meetings ahead of time. For me, it's difficult to not schedule meetings in advance because it doesn't allow me time to prepare or give you the attention you deserve. I am happy to schedule early meetings with you before you meet with customers. Would that be okay with you moving forward? Please obviously still call or text for emergencies and I will respond as promptly as possible."

No triple whammies since.

#3. A client oversteps personal boundaries.

They call you at nine p.m., text you on weekends, DM you on Instagram.

Again, the important thing here is setting boundaries and reinforcing them. Personally, I only communicate with clients via email and phone calls on my business line. So if a client texts me or messages me on social media, I respond with an email saying something along the lines of:

"I received your text/message on Facebook. In the future, will you please email me? This will ensure your message is responded to in a timely manner and not overlooked."

I've even told clients, "I don't check texts during work hours, so I can stay on task. Email is the best way to reach me."

If a client calls me after-hours, I almost always let it go to voicemail. Sometimes, I listen to the voicemail to see if it's an emergency, sometimes I don't. For my first two years in business, I tried answering every call no matter what time of day (or night). At first, I felt like a superhero and clients praised me for being so responsive. But eventually, I grew sick of taking calls during dinner or before I'd even rolled out of bed in the morning. I needed a healthy work-life balance.

One client who hired me early on was an old-school, no-nonsense, no-filter kind of guy. When I first started out, I feared people like this, but over time grew to like them because I always knew where I stood with them. There was never any guessing.

After a week of signing on to our marketing program, I could tell he was going to be a handful. He didn't like to set meetings and expected me to answer whenever he called, no matter what. He said, "If someone calls me, I answer. Period. So I expect the same from you."

I could tell he was frustrated that I wasn't always accessible to him. He called often, sometimes multiple times in a row if I didn't answer, and each time, it was a simple question about his website or marketing strategy. He was driving me crazy! A few weeks into his campaign, he said, "Listen, I'm busy working from eight a.m. to six p.m. I usually don't have time to look at the website until after those hours, and if I call, I expect you to answer."

If this had been my first year in business, I would've said, "Absolutely! No problem."

Instead, I confidently replied, "I don't answer calls after-hours, but if you email me or leave me a voicemail, I'll respond first thing the next morning. I'm very careful to maintain a healthy work-life balance so I can be refreshed and ready to work hard for you during work hours. Does that work for you?"

Truthfully, I thought he might get offended or quit working with us, but he responded with, "Well, you're the boss, so I guess it's gonna have to."

His relationship with our company did a complete 180 after that. He emailed first before calling and only during work hours. I could tell he respected me more for setting the ground rules. After about a month, he completely stopped calling out of the blue and trusted us to handle his marketing campaign.

Set the ground rules without being afraid of losing a client. They'll either learn to respect your boundaries, or they won't and they'll leave. Either way, you win.

#4. A client tries to dictate your schedule.

We once took on a client who sold chocolates online. She was another type-A, tell-you-how-it-is type of person. She had a limited budget and wanted to break into the highly competitive e-commerce chocolate market in California. There were competitors spending $100,000+ on online ads and her budget was less than $5,000. We told her it was an uphill battle, but that we'd do everything we could to try and make it work.

One evening about four weeks into the campaign, I received an angry email about the campaign performance, which ended in, "I'll come to your office tomorrow at 4:30 for a face-to-face, to review what is going on and what has been accomplished."

I couldn't help but laugh. I never let *anyone* dictate my schedule besides me. I replied explaining that I was booked up for the rest of the week, but would be happy to meet in person the following Monday or call between appointments on Friday.

#5. A client screams or curses you out.

A handful of times in my career, a client has totally exploded on me or one of my team members, resulting in screaming, name-calling, cursing. I firmly believe in saying, "Please let me know when you want to talk respectfully." *Click.*

Was this a one-time thing? You may decide to forgive the client and continue the relationship. Is this client a ticking time-bomb? A headache on a good day? Dealing with a person like this is toxic. They drain your energy, which prevents you from feeling motivated to kick ass and limits your financial potential. Think about all the time you spend stressing about a headache client, sending them carefully worded emails, mustering up the courage to call them, losing sleep in extreme cases. When I realized I could attract and service three easy-going clients for the time and energy of one headache client, it made firing them a no-brainer.

The line between success and people-pleasing has blurred many times in my career. I can't tell you how many times I've had to relearn this lesson. Bookmark or mentally flag this chapter. Anytime you are dealing with an unreasonable client, come back and read it.

Chapter 17

Become an Influencer

The best way to solidify your brand in the consumer's mind is to become an influencer. As a refresher, influencers are people who have the clout to influence large numbers of people and impact purchasing decisions via social or traditional media. As my company started to take off, I realized my niche was in the window treatment space. Since my father owned a window treatment store, I grew up in the industry and clients *loved* this. They didn't have to tell me the difference between a blind, shade, shutter, or curtain because I had five years of experience selling those products.

It was important that I scaled this personal experience into company values as our business grew. I had my people learn the products inside and out. I had my account managers work in my father's window treatment showroom as a part of their training. They saw the products in action, took calls, scheduled installations, and learned how to convince walk-in customers to set up an in-home shopping appointment.

Because I was an expert and took the time to make my team members experts, our clients were signing with us and staying long-term. But how could I leverage this to take our company to the next level?

Launching WindowTreatmentWebinar.com

The day I decided to launch our free webinar series for window treatment dealers is the day I solidified my position as an influencer. The ultimate goal was to be a resource to all dealers, whether they were clients or potential clients. I used what I knew and also interviewed my clients, which made them feel quite special. Topics included "How to Close More Window Treatment Sales," "Hiring and Firing for Window Treatment Dealers," and one of my personal favorites, "Run your Business, Don't Let Your Window Treatment Business Run You," where we discussed work-life balance and the unique struggles these dealers face.

The feedback from these webinars was overwhelmingly positive. There were no teasers. I didn't give them a taste and make them pay me for the full course. I put it all on the table, and I didn't make it "salesy" at all. I was adding more value than anyone else in my industry without asking for anything in return. And what did I get? Dealers were begging to sign up left and right. With our exclusivity policy, we only took on one window treatment dealer per city. I can't tell you how many dealers we had freak out when we told them we couldn't do business with them. We started building waiting lists in all major cities of people who wanted to do business with us when a spot "opened up." You know you've built a brand when the sales script is flipped and people are begging to do business with you.

From there, I went on to create YouTube videos in my family's showroom to relate to these dealers in a way that no other brand could. They went viral and the business continued to flood in. I then signed up for a service called Reach150 which allowed me to collect testimonials and build my circle of influence. Leveraging these tools and social media, we became the number one marketing firm for window treatment dealers across the country.

And I'll let you in on a little secret. My webinars looked professional, but if my viewers could see what was behind the screen, they'd see a twenty-five-year-old in footed pajamas sitting on her couch with her dogs.

Fake It 'Til You Make It.

There's a lot of value in making your company appear bigger than it really is. There's nothing wrong with this. It isn't lying, it's inflating.

How to Inflate Your Brand

- **Stop underselling yourself.** When people ask what you do, do you tell them you sell T-shirts on the side? Or do you tell them you're the president of a custom T-shirt enterprise? It may feel goofy at first, but imagine you meet the head of a national association who wants to place an order for 500,000 T-shirts. If you undersell yourself, this person won't even give you the time of day.

9. **Set up domain based emails that give the impression you have multiple departments.** For example, contracts could be sent from sales@yourwebsite.com, support can come from support@yourwebsite.com, and invoicing can be sent from billing@yourwebsite.com. Even if you are the only person who will be answering these emails at first, this still gives the impression that your business is large, flourishing, and, most importantly, professional.

- **Use a virtual voicemail system to play an automated greeting with a company directory when customers call.** You'll look like a multi-million-dollar company, when in reality, you may be a team of three people working remotely from home. You may set it up for callers to press 1 for Sales, 2 for Support, and 3 for Billing, all of which ultimately route to you.

- **If you have a home in one city and an office in another city, tell people you have two offices.** If potential clients think you have two offices, you will project an image of success so great that you've expanded to work in multiple cities. Not only can this function aspirationally for you, you can put this on your website for added clout.

- **Mention your assistant when you can,** even if it's just someone you hired through Fiverr.com for $15/week to help with administrative tasks. CEOs and highly successful people have assistants.

- **Develop your website and invest in professional promotional materials, photography, and videos**. Using sites like Fiverr.com, Upwork.com and 99designs.com, this can be extremely affordable and easy to outsource. If you can afford it, hire a trusted professional.

- **Use "We" instead of "I" on all marketing materials.** Whether you think you're going to be a trailblazing genius like Steve Jobs or not, a team is always going to sound more trustworthy than someone working solo.

- Add certifications, associations, and testimonials to your website and promotional materials. You can't expect someone to hire you if they don't know that you're qualified.

- **Get online reviews.** Lots of them! Nothing instills confidence in potential customers more than hearing about real experiences from real people.

I'll let you in on a little secret. I gave a few examples in the previous chapter on setting boundaries and firing clients. I've had better success than most at setting boundaries with clients *because* I've become an influencer and inflated my brand. People in the window treatment industry know my name and see my ads on social media daily. Demand is high for our services and our exclusivity policy creates a shortage. I can't and won't work with everyone, so when I set boundaries with people, they typically respect them.

As you become an influencer, demand for your brand will grow. And you didn't quit the 9-to-5 to work 24/7. You'll need to build a team of rock stars if you want to scale your business, and in the next chapter, I'll show you how.

Chapter 18

Hire Slow, Fire Fast

There will come a time when you simply can't and shouldn't do everything on your own. When you get to this point, stop and congratulate yourself. You've built something so successful that you can no longer manage it on your own. This is a *huge* accomplishment. Soak it in!

I want to cement the importance of hiring slow and firing fast. Your team will make or break your brand. Most people wait to hire until they're desperate, overworked, and out of steam, so they rush to find help. In doing so, they don't take the time to find a healthy pool of candidates, properly vet each one, thoroughly interview, and test on-the-job skills. They grab the low-hanging fruit and end up with a team of mediocre, last-second hires. Then, when these under-performers start screwing things up, the owner lets them off the hook because they are desperate for help and don't want to go through the entire hiring process again.

If people show their true colors and prove they can't be trusted, fire them *immediately.* Don't let them hang around and drag your brand through the mud. (Now, some underperforming team members just need clear expectations and a kick in the pants in the form of a corrective action plan. When I say fire fast, I'm not talking about those people. I'm talking about firing people who have proven they can't be trusted to represent your brand in a way that no corrective action plan is going to fix.) That being said, if you do your due diligence and hire slow in the first place, chances are, you'll rarely have to fire.

For my first few years in business, I waited to hire until I was completely and totally burned out. I'd work long hours, pull all-nighters, and answer client calls and emails at all hours of the day until I simply couldn't stand it anymore. The cycle would be to work hard because I had to, work harder trying to get ahead, have a mental breakdown when I can't seem to stop falling behind, and finally cave and hire help. Then the cycle would repeat. Here I was convinced I was a professional superhero, when in reality, I lacked vision and wasn't properly planning. I let my business run *me* instead of running my business. Letting yourself get to the point of burnout is a disservice to you, your brand, and your customers.

I'm Slammed So Now Is the Time to Hire, Right?

In some capacity, yes. But we're not going to rush into anything. Hire slow, remember?

Before we venture further into this topic, I want to discuss the hiring phobias many business owners experience.

1. I can't afford to hire.

2. I don't know how to find good people.

3. I don't know how to be an effective manager.

4. What if the person steals my clients or business?

5. I'm too busy to train someone.

While valid concerns, it's important to note that these are limiting thoughts. They yank your business growth to a screeching halt, so it's crucial to stop them in their tracks and change the thoughts you're feeding your mind.

1. You will find free or cheap help until you are ready to bring on employees.

2. You will find great people who are hard workers.

3. You will learn to be an effective leader.

4. You will grow your team without fear, while protecting the company and relationships you've worked hard to build.

5. The time to train someone is *now.*

Why Your First Hire Should Always Be an Assistant

You started your own business, which means you have value to share with others. You have less time to share that value if you're answering emails, taking unexpected calls, picking up dry cleaning, running to the office supply store or the post office—you get the picture. Your time is better spent on income-producing activities.

If you have to work into the late hours of the night just to keep your head above water, you're not a professional superhero—you're doing something wrong. I learned this the hard way. I hired web developers at first, then content writers, then social media managers, then account managers before I ever hired an assistant. Each time I hired, it would help take things off my plate for a couple of weeks or months, then my workload would swell back out of control.

During one of my out-of-control periods, my newest hire put her two weeks in. She'd been with us for less than six months. I was sick over it; I'd have to add her workload on top of mine when I was already drowning. Looking back now, I realize this situation was my fault. I didn't take the time to train her and that made her job stressful, on top of the fact that every time we interacted, I was stressed out because I was overworked. On her last day, she said, "You should really consider hiring an assistant."

How did I not think of this before? I hired an assistant a few weeks later and I can't tell you how much my life improved. For years, I had been "on-call" at all hours of the day and night, constantly checking my email and phone. I don't think I realized how much of a mental and emotional toll this was taking until it was no longer weighing on me.

Looking back, I didn't hire an assistant sooner because it felt frivolous to me. It felt a bit like admitting defeat. "I'm perfectly capable of answering my own emails," I'd stubbornly tell myself as I sat up at two a.m., trying to reply to two hundred-plus messages.

1. How to Get Help When You Can't Afford to Hire Someone

There are so many options for free or inexpensive help, if you can't afford to bring someone on part- or full-time. Now, I know some business owners who would never dare to go this route because "you get what you pay for." While this statement holds true in some situations, I've had great experiences with unpaid interns and cheap contractors. With endless websites and apps available, now is the best time in history to find free or affordable help.

Find an Intern

College students are hungry for real-world experience. You can find free and paid interns so easily using social media, especially if you're in or near a college town. I've also reached out to nearby universities to ask if they have courses which require real-world experience. Currently, I have two free interns who work ten to fifteen hours per week through a program run by the University of Kentucky's College of Communications. Not only have they helped with our workload, but they've brought new perspective

COLLEGE IS BROKEN · 167

and new ideas to the table. In return, they've gained valuable marketing experience which will set them apart as they apply for full-time jobs post-graduation.

If you don't have a nearby college or you can't find something similar to the internship program at the University of Kentucky's College of Communications, use social media. As I write this in 2019, Facebook and Instagram are my main platforms for recruitment. I've considered attending career fairs but found them to be expensive and time-consuming. Why waste my time when I can get applications via email? We always request a résumé and transcript, so we can weed out candidates with low GPAs. I realize GPA isn't always a fair measure of how successful someone will be, but generally, we've found those with higher GPAs work harder and more efficiently. They care about achieving and impressing their superiors. Here is the verbiage we use on Facebook and Instagram when we advertise our internships: "Internship hunting hear Lexington? We're a local agency now hiring social media interns! $10/hour. Work from home on your schedule. Gain fantastic experience managing social media for multiple small businesses."

This ad directs to a simple landing page on our website that is very clean. It requests a name, email and phone number to apply, explaining that we will follow up to request a résumé and transcript once we receive their contact information. We do this because most candidates are seeing the ad on their phone where they don't have this information readily available.

Recently, I ran this ad and spent $35.76, received twenty-two clicks to visit the landing page and received nine applicants to choose from. For the ads, I targeted people ages eighteen to twenty who attend the University of Kentucky and Eastern Kentucky University, the two closest colleges to me.

Fiverr.com

Fiverr.com is a fantastic freelance marketplace where you can hire people to do pretty much anything, starting at $5 per task/service. You can hire graphic designers, web developers, virtual assistants, content writers, video and audio production services, and more. For my first six months in business, it was me, myself, and Fiverr. My clients knew I was a one-woman show and were amazed at how much value I could deliver in such a quick time frame, and much of that speedy turnaround was due to contractors from Fiverr helping me fill the gaps in my time or expertise.

Share a Full-Time Assistant with Friends

Can't afford a full-time assistant? I've heard of lawyers, for example, hiring one assistant who rotates between their offices. With this kind of setup, you can get an assistant for two hours a day on a shoestring budget.

Hiring Contractors on a Project Basis

On many occasions, I've used sites like Upwork.com or 99designs.com to hire contractors for specific projects. If you have a big website you're designing or a graphic design project, you can hire someone for an hourly or fixed rate. You can choose based on numbers of reviews, hours worked, and successful projects completed. I've even maintained long-term relationships with some of the contractors I've met through Upwork.

Hire a Salesperson on a Commission-Only Basis

If you can't afford to pay someone, come up with a commission structure that is enticing for a driven salesperson. Great salespeople love working on commission, if the pay is structured properly. If they grow your business drastically, they should be rewarded handsomely. Be sure to meet with a business consultant to ensure your structure makes sense and is profitable for your business as you grow.

2. How to Find and Hire Great Full-Time People

Full-time employees are a much bigger commitment than freelancers. It's crucial to spend time vetting candidates and making sure you find someone who is trustworthy and hardworking.

When I hired my first full-time employee, outside of remote web developers, I was drowning in work. I needed an Account Manager to step in and take over client relations, which was eating up most of my day. Short on sleep and at my wit's end, I sent out ten messages on LinkedIn to local college seniors in the marketing field. About half responded, and out of those, one really shined on the phone. She was well-spoken, energetic, and friendly, which made her seem like the perfect Account Manager. Her GPA was a hair above a 2.0. I asked her why it was so low and she had a great, honest response. She didn't take her courses as seriously as she should have her first two years. She'd grown up a lot since then and made every effort to raise her GPA during the rest of her education. Then, she stuck the landing with a power statement about her work ethic and that if I had any doubts, she would prove them wrong.

She was the one, no question. I scheduled the in-person interview—a formality at this point because I had already made my decision. She showed up five minutes late but nailed every question. She had a killer personality, which was exactly what I was looking for in an Account Manager. I gave her the job on the spot.

Turns out, despite her communication skills, she was unmotivated, easily distracted, and untrustworthy. She was constantly on her phone, texting or on social media. Tasks that I finished in twenty minutes would take her two hours. Even though she was slow, she was helping with my workload. The idea of replacing her and trying to make the time to re-train someone else felt unbearable at the time. As someone who tries to take responsibility for everything, I told myself, "I need to set the ground rules. I need to be a better leader. I need to learn what motivates her."

You can't motivate someone who doesn't want to be motivated. You can't lead someone who isn't ready to be led. And you can't set ground rules for someone who bends and ignores them.

I made two *huge* mistakes here and I paid for them: I hired fast and I fired slow. I kept her around for over a year, which was hands down the most stressful year of my life. Looking back, I should have cancelled the interview when she showed up five minutes late, or possibly filtered her out in the first place due to GPA.

To help you avoid finding yourself in the situation that I ended up in, let's talk about the five steps to hiring smart and how to master them.

1. Get Crystal Clear About Who You're Looking For

Take the time to write out a job description. When someone asks this person, "What do you do?", it will be their sixty-second elevator pitch. Next, write a sample daily agenda or priority list. What will be on their plate on a day-to-day basis?

After you're crystal clear about the job itself, flesh out the type of person you're looking for. What qualities and skill sets should they have? Write a list in order of priority. (We will use this later to create the interview questions.) This will change based on the job you are hiring for. For example, when we hire Account Managers, their main role is to interact with clients and keep them happy. Therefore, I'm looking for someone with excellent communication skills, someone likable, energetic, friendly, and well-spoken. These are nonnegotiable qualities. With web developers, communication skills aren't nearly as important. Our web developers are behind the scenes, and they almost never speak with clients. Here, my top skill set is development experience.

My other non-negotiable qualities are dependability and work ethic. I'm looking for people who are intrinsically motivated to succeed. They don't need a manager hovering over their shoulder. They thrive in an environment where they have freedom to problem-solve on their own. I can count on them to show up and give it their all, day-in and day-out.

What are your non-negotiable qualities? Remember, while some skills are transferable from position to position, such as dedication and time management, each position is ultimately different. Make sure you have a good handle on what you are hiring for when you think of these qualities, so you know exactly who to look for.

2. Recruit

Now it's time to find those excellent communicators and hard workers. We've always found candidates effortlessly online using the following methods:

Social Media

- Facebook and Instagram ads have been tremendously effective. Our full-time ads are pretty similar to the ads for interns. We ask a question like, "Job hunting in Lexington?" Then, we insert a brief statement about who we're looking for and highlight the perks. We typically also insert an application deadline two weeks from the start date, so candidates don't drag their feet. Here is the exact verbiage we used to hire our last Account Manager: "Job hunting in Lexington? We're now hiring a full-time Mar-

keting Strategist/Account Manager. Creekmore Marketing is a fast-growing company with plenty of opportunity
for growth. Apply now!"

- Make the landing page for your ad simple, quick to load,
  and enticing. Be sure to include salary. We get way more
  applications when we're upfront with this information.

- I used to post personally on social media about open positions but stopped because I don't want to ruin relationships with friends and family members. Don't get me
  wrong; I've found lots of great, trustworthy individuals
  that I already knew who made great additions to our
  team. But I've also hired family members I've had to end
  up firing for poor performance. This ends up being uncomfortable for everyone, so I would recommend avoid-
  ing it altogether.

- Make it a rule to never hire close friends. Nothing ruins a
  relationship like becoming your best friend's superior and
  cutting their paychecks.

- I've found many team members through sites like Up-
  work.com or Outsourcely.com. These sites allow you to
  select candidates with specific skill sets, read their reviews, and interview them if you think they're a good fit
  for your position. Upwork even has built-in time tracking
  software and a payment system, which makes everyone's
  life easy.

- Ask people in your community. I found my salesperson
  through a local networking meeting completely by
  chance. You never know when you're going to meet that
  person who takes your business to the next level.

3. Phone Interview

The next stage is to schedule a phone interview. At this stage, I have a list of ten to fifteen questions, which help me identify the qualities this person has and if I think they would be a good fit for the position.

I was so awkward during my first few interviews; I swear, I was more nervous than the interviewee. I bumbled out a hello, then started grilling them with questions. I've learned since to chat with the person and give them a little bit of background information on our company and the position before jumping into the questions.

Here is my standard list of phone interview questions:

- Tell me a little bit about yourself.

- How did you hear about the position?

- What is your greatest professional strength?

- What is your biggest weakness? (*I know these questions are cliché, but they work. I had multiple interviewees tell me things like, "I have trouble staying focused," or, "I have a hard time crossing things off my to-do lists," to which I cringed so hard that I cut the interview short, and thanked them for their time.*)

- How do you deal with stressful situations?

- Tell me about a conflict at school or work and how you overcame it.

- Where do you see yourself in five years?

- How do you stay focused throughout the workday/avoid distraction?

- Why do you want this job?

- Why should we hire you over the other candidates who have applied?

- Do you have any questions for me?

When I hire Account Managers, the phone interview stage is crucial. I'm looking for people who really wow me on the phone because most of our clients are out of state and solely communicate with us via calls. I can't tell you how many soon-to-be graduates I've interviewed who sounded bored on the phone. At that point, it didn't really matter to me what they said. They were missing a non-negotiable.

Time Hack: If communication skills are a non-negotiable for you, set up a free Google Voice line at https://voice.google.com. Then, whenever you get an applicant whose résumé/transcript fits your criteria, send them this email:

Thank you for applying for our *** position! The next step in the interview process is to call and leave a message on our Google Voice line explaining why you want this job. I know it sounds goofy, but a majority of client communication in this position is over the phone. Your ability to sound friendly, yet professional is a crucial skill.

The number is (859) 333-3333. Please let me know when this is complete.

Thanks!

Chelsea Creekmore
CEO
Creekmore Marketing

This allows you to weed out anyone who doesn't have the enthusiasm or communication skills you need. Each time I've hired for this position, I've been buried in work, and I would get so frustrated when I would block out hours of my day to interview people who sounded unenthused. Problem solved!

4. In-Person Interview

Next, it's time to meet your best candidates in person and narrow down from there. Don't jump to this stage too soon. If you haven't found anyone that wowed you on the phone, keep looking.

If you don't have an office yet, meet candidates at a local coffee shop for the interview. Arrive twenty minutes early and pay attention to the time the candidate arrives. Early is ideal, on-time, average, and late, no longer in the running, even if it's just a minute. No excuses. If that person was willing to waste even a moment of your time during the interview process, the time they should be going above and beyond to impress you, something's wrong.

Here is my round-two list of questions. You can use some of these or formulate your own using your quality list.

- Why are you leaving your current job? (If applicable.)

- Why is there a gap in your employment? (If applicable.)

- What are you looking for in a new position?

- What types of projects or tasks do you enjoy most?

- What type of work environment do you prefer?

- Tell me about a time you exercised leadership.

- How would your manager or coworkers describe you?

- What makes you a good communicator?

- If your workload is overwhelming, how do you handle that?

- Do you have any questions for me?

To me, it is a huge strike in the candidate's "no" column if they don't ask me questions at the end. If you haven't interviewed before, you'll understand when you do. The most impressive candidates pick your brain at the end of the interview to show they care about your company and want to be prepared for the opportunity.

I wait until I have two incredible candidates to choose from before I think about offering the job. This forces me to make a difficult decision and typically extends the hiring process but is well worth it. On multiple occasions, I've thought I've found "the one," only to interview someone the next day and find they are more impressive and more qualified.

When selecting your top candidate, remember, just because you like someone does not mean they will be a good fit for your position. We often like people who share similar personality traits and values to us. Sometimes you need someone with the *opposite* personality type and values because they will excel in your areas of weakness. Remember the CVI assessment I mentioned in chapter 4? I recommend utilizing this tool in your hiring process for key employees. For example, I'm a Merchant-Innovator, so I need Builders and Bankers around me for our company to thrive. You'll want to avoid putting people in roles that conflict with their core values. For example, I have virtually no Banker in me. If I were applying for an accounting job, I could probably land it with my interviewing skills, but would be *miserable* day-to-day. I would drive my manager crazy because I'm not a detail-oriented, analytical person. I should be in a position that plays to my strengths, relationship-building and innovation, rather than one that forces me to operate in my area of weakness. Having your top candidates take a CVI assessment before hiring them could save you months or years of frustration.

5. Offer the Position

Don't just assume the person will accept your offer. I've called someone and excitedly shared the good news, "You got the job!", only to be awkwardly turned down. "I found another position that offers benefits." Yikes. (This was before we offered benefits as a company.)

Call your top candidate, offer the position, and sell that person on why they should accept. Get them excited about the opportunity for growth, the experience, the perks. Then ask, "Would you like a day to think about it before you give me an answer?"

Ever since I started selling candidates and giving them time to accept, I'm hardly ever turned down.

3. How to Be an Effective Leader

As a child, I exhibited many qualities of a leader. If we were playing a game, I was the commissioner. If we were filming a movie or putting on a play, I was the director. This carried throughout my educational career, as I often took the lead on projects and wasn't afraid to speak up in class. Surely, I'd make a great manager, right?

Wrong.

Throughout my first few years in business, I failed *miserably* as a leader. I didn't train my team well. I was scared to teach my employees too much about my business, so I limited the information I shared, which stunted their growth and made them ill-equipped to interact with clients. Once, a client asked one of my employees how much her monthly bill was and the employee had no idea. The client was so upset that she ended up switching to another marketing firm. Looking back, I can't say I blame her!

On top of this, my team could tell I didn't fully trust them, which hurt my ability to lead and inspire them. I was afraid to directly challenge them when their performance was poor, so instead I pretended everything was peachy and simply tried to praise everyone for the good things they did, in hopes it would somehow motivate them.

I'd say, "Nice job on the website project today!" when really, I was thinking, Nice job, you finally found time to work on the website after messing around on your phone for two hours!

This killed my effectiveness as a leader, because it encouraged the lazy workers to continue messing around on their phones, and it frustrated the hell out of the hard workers. If I was just going to praise everyone anyway, why shouldn't everyone take a two-hour Candy Crush break?

This environment was mentally and emotionally draining for me. I felt constantly frustrated and resentful at work. I didn't have the time or energy to groom my best team members because I was busy picking up the slack from the lazy ones.

At the end of the day, my team found their jobs frustrating, uncomfortable, and unfulfilling. I lost team members I would have loved to keep around because of my flaws as a leader. This stunted the growth of the business and caused endless headaches, but at the time, I simply couldn't figure out why. Then, one day during a layover at the airport, I stumbled across the book *Radical Candor* by Kim Scott[34]. She shares an eye-opening graphic which explains the four leadership approaches:

- A leader who is blunt without caring personally shows Obnoxious Aggression.

- A leader who sugarcoats things without caring personally shows Manipulative Insincerity.

- A leader who sugarcoats things while caring personally shows Ruinous Empathy.

- A leader who is blunt while caring personally is Radically Candid.

This book opened my eyes to my fatal leadership flaws, which were my tendencies to show Ruinous Empathy or Manipulative Insincerity. Becoming Radically Candid was a total gamechanger for me. I fired my worst team members. Some of my best team members left for other jobs, despite my attempts to repair those relationships. I worked eighty-hour weeks to pick up the slack. I was scrambling to find new talent, yet determined to avoid the mistakes I made the first time around.

While this was one of the most stressful times in my business, it resulted in an incredible shift in our company culture. I was radically candid with the new hires from day one. I set the bar high, trained them well, and provided direct feedback every step of the way. My team was happier and working ten times harder for me, because I earned their respect.

I can't tell you how wrong I was to think it would be easier to sugarcoat things with my team instead of facing problems head-on. While it may seem challenging in the moment to be direct with people, especially when providing criticism, push past those uncomfortable feelings and be honest.

Don't make the same mistakes I did. Don't avoid giving criticism because it's uncomfortable. Being direct with your team is a critical step in scaling your company.

No matter how busy you are, never be too busy for the key people in your organization. This is a balancing act. After all, you hired people to take things off your plate, not add to it, right? The more you scale your business, the less you'll be involved in the day-to-day. Therefore, you must get your team to buy into your vision. People buy into the leader before they even consider the vision, and ultimately, people buy into leaders who buy into them. Buy into your team members so that they will buy into you, and the vision you have for your company. It's as simple as that.

Believe in each of your team members. See their weaknesses as opportunities for growth. Take time out of your busy schedule to invest in training them and helping them grow as leaders. Show them how you put out fires and deal with problem clients without breaking a sweat. And most importantly, stay relentlessly positive.

Strengthening your leadership muscle takes time. The best leaders in the world stay hungry and constantly learn new ways to inspire others. One book or video or class won't do the trick. Commit to consistently developing yourself as a leader.

4. How to Grow Your Team without Fear and Protect Your Business

Find a local attorney and invest in a good employment contract. If you're going to hire, do it right and *don't* complain that you can't afford it. If you can afford to pay someone, you can afford an attorney.

It's crucial to include a non-compete, non-solicitation, and a confidentiality agreement. You may consider patent protection for your business method(s), should your attorney feel this is appropriate.

Non-Compete

Non-compete agreements prevent employees from leaving your company to work for a competitor or start their own competing business. These can be difficult to enforce and must be considered "reasonable" in the eyes of the court. The more selective you are about the duration and location, the better. For example, you'll have a much better chance of enforcing a six-month non-compete within your state than you would a three-year national non-compete.

Non-Solicitation

This kills two birds with one stone. It prevents employees from soliciting your customers after they leave, as well as trying to take other employees with them.

Confidentiality

This agreement prevents employees from sharing your trade secrets, customer lists, and other business practices with others. You can also have vendors and suppliers sign these agreements.

Patent Protection

You may consider filing a patent for your business practices. The US Patent Office has been known to grant these, especially if your business practices fall into the internet/high tech realm.

Intellectual Property

Include a clause stating any intellectual property created by the employee throughout the course of employment is your property.

I know I mentioned how dangerous it can be to keep your employees in the dark. You must fully trust them and not be afraid to disclose information about your business that is necessary for them to properly perform their jobs. That being said, you can still disclose on a need-to-know basis.

Train your team on everything you think they need to know and then foster an environment of openness, so they're not hesitant to ask for more information when they need it. I regularly ask my team if there is anything they are confused about that I can clear up. I also have them keep a list of "curveball" questions clients have thrown their way, so I can teach them how to respond and better train future team members.

5. How to Train Someone When You're So Busy You Can't See Straight

"I'm too busy to train someone" are the famous last words of entrepreneurs who fail to seize their moment. You will always be too busy to train someone until you train someone. You may not have the time, but you need to make the time. The good news is, you don't have to spend weeks babysitting this person while the rest of your work piles up. Here are four key tips to help you train someone without having a breakdown:

- **Shadowing**. Have him or her tag along as you perform your regular duties for a few weeks. Even if their role will be different than the job you're performing, it will be helpful for them to understand the ins and outs of your business. I often had employees shadow me half the day and write down absolutely everything I did and said. Then, they'd spend the second half of the day studying, reorganizing, or retyping their notes, in addition to working on other small projects.

- **Give them projects they can take on right away.** If you've done a good job hiring, your employee is excited and ready to work hard for you. Let them know how busy you are and how much it would help if they could start by taking some "housekeeping" projects off your plate. Make a list of things you've been meaning to do, like organizing your office, moving your customer list to a new CRM (Customer Relationship Management) platform, or updating your website or social media profiles. Write down every possible project you can think of. Even if it doesn't sound like a good project for a newbie, you may want to get help with it down the road once your employee is more familiar with your business and customers.

- **Have them drum up new business.** Get them to join a local networking group, such as BNI (www.bni.com). Have them call, email, or write letters to previous customers to encourage repeat and referral business. They could start an email marketing campaign, take photos of your products or projects and put them online, write a blog post, create a YouTube video, develop relationships with local businesses in complementary industries and see if they'd be interested in a referral program, help you get online reviews, and deal with any lingering negative reviews.

Don't be afraid to let your new hire jump in and get their hands dirty. They might make mistakes at first and that's okay. If you're too afraid to hand the reins over, your workload will continue to spiral out of control.

Now you know how to find free or cheap help until you are ready to bring on employees, how to develop yourself as a leader, grow your team while protecting your company, and why "too busy to hire" is a sign that now is actually the perfect time to hire.

184 · CHELSEA CREEKMORE

Boss's Action Plan:

1. As your workload grows, proactively plan your next five hires. As you plan these roles, do so in a way that allows you to focus on your strengths and delegate your weaknesses, as well as anything you hate doing. In many cases, an assistant should be your first hire. Your next may be an unpaid intern, commission-only salesperson, and project-based contractors. If cash flow allows and the workload is there, perhaps these positions need to be full-time hires.

2. Run ads on social media, or use sites like Fiverr.com, Upwork.com, Outsourcely.com, or 99designs.com to find help. Ask around in your local community, but tread carefully when it comes to hiring friends and family members.

3. Find a local attorney and invest in a good employment contract.

4. Go slowly through the hiring process. Vet each candidate carefully, and don't choose someone until you have at least two people who have really wowed you. Use the CVI assessment to ensure their core values and strengths will be frequently utilized in their job role, and they won't be forced to operate in their area of weakness too often.

5. If you're too busy to train your people, have them shadow you, take on housekeeping projects or tasks they can figure out themselves, and network to drum up new business.

6. If a team member is unmotivated, breaks your trust, or shows they can't handle the responsibility you've given them, fire fast. No matter how busy you are, fire this person and find a replacement. There is no greater peace of

mind than finding a team member you wholeheartedly trust and know will always do right by you.

7. Develop yourself as a leader. Commit to reading a book or taking a course on leadership this month. Interview friends and family members who manage employees. What do they like/dislike about being a manager? What are their biggest struggles? What do they wish they knew when they first started managing people? Interview five people and learn from their experience.

Now that you know how to build an unstoppable team, massive success is well within your reach. In the next chapter, we'll discuss the resistance you'll face as you level up from friends, family, and haters.

Chapter 19

The Pull

When you really start leveling up, you're going to feel "the pull" from others in your life who want to bring you back to their level. Oftentimes, the pull is not malicious. It's simply your friends and family members wanting to connect with you. Let's say you used to go out partying every weekend with your friends. You wake up on Saturday or Sunday mornings (or both) feeling like death. You feel unhealthy, unmotivated, perhaps guilty or embarrassed about things you said or did the night before. You know, deep down, partying is preventing you from reaching your full potential.

So, you make the decision to stop. You know you're making the best choice for your health, wealth, and future, but your friends don't see it that way. So, what do they do? They tease you, call you lame, and tell you you've changed.

They're not doing this out of malice; they just want you to be back on their level.

It's hard to be a different person around the same people. You've got to sell yourself a thousand percent on your decisions and develop rock-solid assurance and confidence around them. As the saying goes, "You're under no obligation to be the same person you were 5 minutes ago."

Let Your Haters Inspire You

Inevitably, people will get jealous of you. It's human nature to envy those with bigger bank accounts, careers, and aspirations.

My haters told me:

- "There are so many books out there. Do you really think yours will get published?"

- "Online business communities are overdone. Don't even bother."

And once my business gained national recognition, I started getting comments online like, "This lady is a crook. She out-sources her work to China." (Not true.)

I eat it up when people doubt me. It's like someone tossing lighter fluid on my fire. Every time it happened throughout my career, I'd write it down and tell myself, "I'm going to remember this when I make it big."

People pull others down because it makes them feel better. It's not about you; it's about their insecurities.

Stand Strong or Push Away?

When you feel the pull from others, you must decide whether you want to stand strong or push away. Pushing away from re-lationships with particularly strong pulls may be necessary. Standing strong involves keeping the relationships in your life but refusing to be dragged down.

You can still love the people in your life who disagree with your path or don't buy into your vision, but you also have the right to push away if you feel that's the best decision for your future. Each time you level up, commit to taking fewer and fewer opinions. You may find your circle of influence gets smaller as your dreams get bigger.

Elevate Your Circle of Influence

It's so important to surround yourself with people who inspire you. Ask around or find people online who share your dream. When writing this book, I asked everyone I knew until I found another young author who was willing to meet with me and let me pick his brain. The conversation was incredible because we connected instantly and deeply through our shared passion of writing.

I left the meeting feeling so incredibly energized that I wanted more. So, I decided to create a mastermind group for young entrepreneurs called Bosses and Breadwinners. My local chapter meets twice per month to inspire each other and hold each other accountable for our goals. When I met these people, the connection was instant and palpable because we had so much in common. These entrepreneurs understood my struggles, shared my ambition, and have since become some of my dearest friends. I now have an unofficial board of directors to run ideas by and get feedback from when I'm feeling stuck. Lastly, I can't even describe to you how confident I feel knowing I have a tribe of people locally who have my back and are cheering me on every step of the way. You can learn more at www.bossesandbreadwinners.com if you're interested in starting your own local mastermind group.

Beware of the Most Dangerous Hater: You

The most dangerous pull of all comes from the hater that lives in your head. The one who says, "You're not good enough." "Who do you think you are?" "Do you really think you can become a millionaire?"

In the next section, we'll discuss how to become hyper-aware of your negative self-talk and flip the switch whenever it happens. When your mind says, "Do you really think your business will be successful?" respond with, "I'll do whatever it takes to make my business successful. I'm going to have so many clients, I'll have to turn people away. Money flows easily and effortlessly into my life."

You're a boss. You've got mountains to move. You don't have the time or energy to mess with self-doubt or people who drag you down. Resist the pull and level up without apology.

Phase 3

Finding Joy In The Journey

Chapter 20

Creating Joy

No matter what your dreams are, your ultimate goal in life is to be happy. Am I right? Cars, clients, and career accomplishments provide temporary excitement, but not lasting fulfillment. Learning to create your own joy is a competitive advantage in the business world. For most, the entrepreneurial journey is filled with failure, disappointment, haters, and months or *years* of being broke. People may doubt you, look down upon you, and tear you down, simply because you're doing what they're too afraid to do—follow their dreams.

Let's be real—even if you earn seven figures, a million dollars is *worthless* if you're miserable. So let's talk about how to create a happy life.

For most, a happy life consists of:

- Fully accepting and loving yourself for who you are.

- Fully accepting where you are in life, even if you are hungry for more.

- Being yourself.

- Saying no to things, people, and events that don't serve you.

- Taking ample time to rest, explore, and enjoy the presence of the people you love.

- Pursuing your passions and following your dreams on a daily basis, even if it's just baby steps.

- Not worrying about hurting other people's feelings.

- Feeling your emotions instead of suppressing them.

- Releasing your expectations and taking nothing personally.

- Being honest and direct, even when it causes conflict. (Sugarcoating to avoid conflict may feel like a happiness technique, but it's quite the opposite because you aren't being true to yourself and your feelings.)

- Developing a rock-solid confidence in yourself and your abilities.

- Learning to ignore your negative thoughts and cut out toxic influences from your life.

- Surrounding yourself with people who love you and make you feel important.

- Learning how to make everyone around you feel important.

- Being vulnerable and making mistakes without letting it hurt your confidence.

We don't just want to be happy every now and then; we want to feel joy, excitement, and fulfillment on a day-to-day basis. We do not feel we've achieved a happy life if said happiness is not consistent.

I want you to stop right now and do an exercise for me. This will be a weeklong, quick and easy journaling exercise. You'll answer questions before you go to bed at the end of each day. Was today a good day or bad day? If it was a good day, why?

And if it was a bad day, why? Many of us find that there are multiple reasons why we judge the day as good or bad, so feel free to make a list.

Do not try to outsmart this exercise. It is effective when you're honest with yourself about how you think and feel about each day. There are no wrong answers and no points for having more good days than bad. If you have more bad days than good days, it doesn't mean something is wrong with you.

I'm going to share examples next, so if you haven't completed this exercise yet, I challenge you to pause where you are in this book and come back in a week.

Look at what you've written over the past week and tell me how many of your good days were caused by external factors. For example, I had a good day because I didn't get caught in traffic, and it was sunny, and I didn't have to put out any fires at work. The person in front of me at Starbucks bought my coffee and I was excited to come home at the end of the night and read a book I'm really into right now. Maybe you had a bad day because your electric bill was $75 more expensive than you thought it would be this month. Maybe your manager yelled at you or you're in a fight with your significant other.

Look at each and every one of these reasons and know that these are the things you are allowing to dictate your happiness. If any of these are external, then your happiness relies on whether or not something goes your way. Therefore, your happiness will never be consistent because you cannot control other people or outside circumstances. It's like trying to reach a destination with a broken compass. It simply won't happen.

Knowing that consistent happiness is the goal, we must vow to gauge our happiness based on things within our control.

Now, I can feel some of you rolling your eyes. "Yeah, happiness is in my control. Easier said than done." This is a totally fair reaction. I've felt this way many times in my life.

Gen Kelsang Nyema is an American Buddhist nun who spoke at the 2014 TEDxGreenville conference. The exercise you just participated in was inspired by her talk. I'd like to quote one particular part because it is simple, yet profound. It really sunk in for me when I was feeling skeptical about cultivating inner happiness. She said:

Happiness and unhappiness are states of mind. Therefore, their real causes cannot be found outside the mind. If we have a peaceful state of mind, we will be happy regardless of people and circumstances. If our mind is unpeaceful or agitated, then even if we have really good circumstances, we'll find it impossible to be happy. So, in other words, it's not what is happening that is making us happy or unhappy. It is how we are responding to those things that determines whether we are happy or unhappy.[35]

The real key to cultivating long-term happiness is to realize we are in control of how we react, and we can train our brains to choose peace in the most tumultuous situations. You must wholeheartedly believe happiness is a choice and a mental state of mind you can cultivate. If you're currently holding onto any skeptical thoughts, release them. This is the biggest obstacle holding you back from the consistent happiness you desire. And I'm not speaking to people with clinical depression here. There is a clear difference between people with a neurochemical deficiency and those who choose to be unhappy. That being said, happiness is available to anyone with enough work and introspection, even those with depression or other mental illnesses. Your journey may include medical, therapeutic, and/or holistic remedies, and that's perfectly fine. The bravest thing you can do is to ask for help when you can't help yourself.

As a boss, you are taking responsibility for your happiness. You refuse to let others or outside circumstance be in the driver's seat of your life. I want to congratulate you, because once you fully embrace this truth, you will find deeper fulfillment in your life than any level of success will bring you.

And while this book is about walking the path to seven figures, that is not the only form of success. Success may be making enough money to pay the bills and put food on the table, while allowing you the freedom to set your own schedule. Maybe success for you is five or six figures. Maybe it's a career that allows you to pursue your passion. It's important to develop a success mind-set and cultivate gratitude for where you are now in life — *today*. And realize, you can simultaneously feel appreciative of where you are in life and also be hungry for more. The two are not mutually exclusive.

Have a Quarter-Life Crisis

Don't wait until halfway through your life to realize you've wasted half your life. Many college grads have said they're having a "quarter-life crisis." I love this! It means we're waking up and stepping down from the corporate ladder to rock-climb our way through life. We are saying no to the debt our parents drowned in, no to doing things that don't serve us, no to spending time with people who drain our energy. There is no more worthy cause than discovering what makes you happy in life. Happy people make other people happy and change the world.

If the corporate world feels soul-sucking to you, choose a different career path or put up with it for a while and start a side business. The future waits for no one, so start pursuing what you love today. Don't waste another twenty-four hours.

You can do one of two things after a mid- or quarter-life crisis: grow or get stuck.

If you choose to get stuck, you may stay in a dead-end job or unhealthy relationship. You may continue living your life on other people's terms instead of your own. You may get lost in addiction, anxiety, or depression. But know that getting stuck is a choice. You are not a product of your circumstances; your circumstances are a product of your decisions and your attitude.

If you choose to grow from your midlife crisis, here is the typical outcome:

- You change career paths

- You get serious about your dreams

- You commit to improving or refreshing a bad relationship

- You leave a toxic relationship

- You spend more time with your loved ones

- You take fewer opinions

- You start speaking your mind

- You make yourself a top priority

A mid-life crisis isn't something that *might* happen to you as you get older. It's a coined term in our society because everyone experiences it; so why not choose growth now?

Chapter 21

Widely Accepted Lies

In our last chapter we talked about ways to cultivate joy. When you cultivate something, it also means getting rid of the things that don't serve you, so in this chapter we'll talk about ridding yourself of things that generate unhappiness. We are going to discuss four widely accepted lies that make most college graduates miserable after graduation, and the importance of rejecting these notions.

The Lie of Finding Your "Life's Purpose"

"Find your purpose in life and you'll be happy." How many times have we heard this, especially when it comes to choosing a career path? For some people, the stars align and they discover a higher calling to dedicate their life to some vocation, goal, or movement. Don't get me wrong; I think that's fantastic. But most college graduates have *no clue* what their purpose is. And guess what? That's completely fine.

You don't need to discover your life's purpose to determine your career path. Like I said, you may *never* find a clear purpose. Life is messy, and higher callings don't always come to us in the form of acceptance letters to wizarding school or having to avenge the death of our fathers.

Discover Your Passion

What do you like to do? What gets you excited? What projects have you worked on that have made time feel like it's flying by? Identify your passions and pursue them relentlessly. They may change over time and that's perfectly fine, but following your passions will always lead you where you need to go.

You can find purpose in each and every day by changing your attitude. People who find purpose in the smallest of things experience the greatest happiness in life.

One of the happiest people I've ever met was a man who worked as a cashier at a local grocery store. Each time I'd see him, he'd greet me with a huge grin, some days a song, and without fail, a corny joke. I asked him how he was so happy all the time and he said, "I just like to make people smile." And he really did, for hundreds of people every day. He made it his mission to pry a smile out of even the grumpiest of folks. What an incredible difference he was making in the world in a job that most college grads consider menial. And he did this with two deformed hands—a disability that would have stopped most people in their tracks.

Find purpose in your everyday life and know that you can make a difference with something as simple as a smile.

The Lie of "Having Your Life All Figured Out"

After graduation, there is this unspoken pressure to have your life "all figured out." Have you felt it? It is as omnipresent as the air you breathe and is perpetuated by social media.

But it's important to remember that social media is not a representation of real life; it is a highlight reel of everyone's best and most beautiful moments, and often it has very little in common with reality. If you allow yourself to buy into this pressure, and then log on and see all these carefully chosen, airbrushed photos of your friends graduating with medical degrees, landing high-paying jobs, buying their first house, or getting married or having kids, it's human nature to develop a sense of inferiority.

Social media isn't the root cause; it simply intensifies the problem of comparing yourself to others and feeling inferior. That being said, social media is an important medium for connection and success in today's world. So how do you utilize this tool without wreaking emotional havoc on yourself? Unfollow every person, brand, or account who makes you feel inferior.

Cutting out the following toxic social influences made a monumental difference in my happiness:

- **Famous people with perfect bodies.** For a time in my life, I considered plastic surgery because I was following stars with implants, tummy tucks, and nose jobs. It filled up my social news feed until one day when I got sick of it and unfollowed everyone that made me feel less beautiful. Now, every day, I make the conscious choice to love my body as it is. It became so much easier when I stopped looking up to people with unrealistic or augmented bodies.

- **Comedic accounts that feel relatable but perpetuate negative beliefs and unhealthy habits.** I followed many accounts that would post relatable memes for college students and recent grads about how much "adulting" sucks, how I'll never get out of debt, and how wine for breakfast is the answer. They were hilarious, don't get me wrong, but encouraged me to continue drinking copious amounts of alcohol, overspending, and being lazy. As I said before, what you feed your mind, you eventually believe, and your beliefs dictate your actions, which creates your circumstances, and ultimately, your life. Do you want your life to be mediocre and comically relatable, or to be happy even if it's less funny? The choice is yours.

- **Negative people**. I unfollowed any negative person, even if they were a close friend or family member, without feeling bad or guilty. I found it crucial to cut out everyone and everything that didn't motivate me to go after my dreams.

Who do I follow now? Bosses in the business and financial world, such as Peter Voogd, Mark Lack, Grant Cardone, Tim Ferriss, Carrie Green, John Maxwell, and Dave Ramsey, to name a few. I unfollow negative people or people who make me feel inadequate. As a boss, I take very few opinions and choose carefully what I feed my brain.

"Comparison Is the Thief of Joy." – Unknown

My life has been exponentially better since I stopped playing the comparison game. There will always be someone prettier, richer, funnier, more fit, or more successful than you. Participating in this game is setting yourself up for failure and misery. There is no shortage of success in this world. Another person's gain is not your loss and life is *not* a competition.

Repeat this mantra. "I wholeheartedly accept where I am in life and commit to finding joy in the journey. I'm a good person. I'm proud of myself and my accomplishments. I'm genuinely happy for others and their accomplishments. The only person I'm competing against is the person I was yesterday."

Did it feel good or phony? If it felt good, say it again. If it felt phony, say it ten more times. Slowly. Believe it more and more each time you say it. The amazing thing about your mind is that you have the power to control it. If you tell it to believe something enough times, it will believe.

If nothing else, promise yourself you will stop comparing your life to others' and see how much your life improves. Constantly monitor your thoughts and stop yourself whenever you start to feel that pit of inferiority in your stomach. Know that you are *exactly* where you're supposed to be in life. Take a big deep breath and release the picture-perfect image of how you think your life "should" be and embrace it for what it is. Stay hungry for more, yes, but learn to cultivate gratitude for where you are today, and don't discount all the things you've accomplished in your life. Bosses *refuse* to give in to societal norms and pressures.

As Mark Twain said, "Whenever you find yourself on the side of the majority, it's time to reform."[36]

The Lie that Success = Happiness

As I said before, just because someone is successful does not mean they're happy. There are plenty of stars and CEOs who are rich and miserable. This is another trick comparison plays on our brains. We convince ourselves that if we were doing as well as so-and-so, or had a body like so-and-so, or had a job like so-and-so, or had as much money as so-and-so, we would achieve "happiness." But, as we learned in the previous chapter, happiness is not a goal or a destination. It is a state of mind that comes from within.

Happiness is minimizing the difference between expectations and reality. If we expect nothing in life, two amazing things happen: we don't feel the sting of disappointment and we can only be pleasantly surprised. One of the biggest disappointments college grads experience is the reality of their first job. We hear these inspiring speeches at graduation and encouraging words from our friends and family members. We've spent our entire adolescent lives preparing for the "real world" and expect our degree will have earned us jobs on our career path that are enjoyable and fulfilling. But for a majority of people, this is not the case. Many struggle to make it through the hiring process, or land a job and then find it's comprised of tedious, entry-level work. Now, I'm not saying you won't find a job you love right off the bat; I'm saying don't expect to. If you're pleasantly surprised, awesome! If not, that's perfectly fine. Take the experience for what it is. You'll get to meet new people and build relationships, some of which may be lifelong connections or friends. You'll learn what you hate in a job so you can build your career around the things you love in the future. I promise there is a silver lining, even if you have to squint to see it.

The Lie of Setting "Realistic" Goals

How many times have people in your life told you to be "realistic" and set "realistic goals"? Ninety-nine percent of the time, the people giving this advice wish deep down they hadn't taken it themselves. You see, you shouldn't fear setting your goals too high; you should fear setting them too low and achieving them. The latter is far riskier and could lead to a life of settling.

> *"Winners are not afraid of losing. But losers are.*
> *Failure is part of the process of success. People*
> *who avoid failure also avoid success."*
> *– Robert T. Kiyosaki[37]*

How many times have you failed this week? You may need to step up your game. The happiest entrepreneurs learn to persist through failure after failure without beating themselves up. This ironclad confidence is not only a competitive advantage in the business world, but one of the biggest keys to lasting joy.

The Lie of Retiring Young

When I've asked students about their wildest dreams, many have said, "To make so much money I can retire at forty and move to the beach." Sounds like the dream, right?

Imagine yourself actually doing this for six months straight— waking up in paradise with nothing to do. For the first few weeks, it would be absolute bliss. But there are only so many days you can spend lounging on the beach before the margaritas taste dull and the sand stuck to your skin starts to drive you mad. "Too much of a good thing" is a saying for a reason. Have you ever been excited to come home at the end of a vacation?

Or, let's just say you didn't move to the beach, but you were so financially set you didn't have to work for money. You could have a lazy Sunday afternoon every day! Awesome, right?

Having no responsibilities quickly loses its luster. That's why it's hard on parents when their children leave the nest. That's why retirees feel lost after a few months of trying to entertain themselves while everyone else goes to work or school. Once the burnout wears off, they're bored as hell.

According to the Federal Reserve, one-third of people who retire eventually go back to work part- or full-time. Many go back for financial reasons, but I don't think we realize how many go back to work because retirement isn't all it's cracked up to be, or how many of the two-thirds would go back to work if they were able.[38] We need purpose and companionship. My grandpa put it bluntly: "When you get old, your kids don't need you and all your friends start dying." Ouch. Couple that with twiddling your thumbs all day and you've got a recipe for depression.

Is early retirement a nail in the coffin?

A study of Shell Oil employees found workers who retire at age 55 are 89 percent more likely to die during the ten years post retirement than workers who retire at 65.[39]

Is it because those who retired early were already sick? Not necessarily. A study at Oregon State University found that both healthy and unhealthy people lived longer as they continued to work.[40]

My grandparents have been very successful in their careers. They could go without working another day in their lives. But my Nina practices real estate and my Papa works at a gun store part-time making a whopping nine dollars an hour. Why? Because she loves selling houses and he loves guns. They have places to be and people who need them to be there. They're happier, healthier, and more social than a majority of people their age.

You don't need to retire young; you need a job that doesn't feel like work. Personally, I will be writing books and running or investing in businesses until the day I die. These careers allow me to set my own schedule; I can work ten-hour days or thirty-minute days. When I want to travel, I can book an international flight at the drop of a hat. When I feel like I haven't gotten enough R&R, I can take a long nap or book a day at the spa. And I'll have a better shot at not missing my future child's basketball games because I "have to work."

Don't count down the days until your retirement. Build a life you don't need to retire from.

Boss's Action Plan:

1. Release any preconceived notions you held about finding your life's purpose. Explore your passions and learn to find purpose in everyday life.

2. Stop comparing yourself to others. Unfollow anyone who makes you feel inferior about yourself and follow those who inspire you. Know you are exactly where you are supposed to be in life.

3. Success does not equal happiness. In fact, success and happiness are states of mind. Eliminate your expectations and you'll often find yourself pleasantly surprised.

4. You shouldn't fear setting your goals too high; you should fear setting them too low and achieving them. Fail often

COLLEGE IS BROKEN · 207

without letting your confidence take a hit. Losers quit when they fail. Winners fail until they succeed.

5. Build a life you don't need to retire from. Remember my challenge to set a quit date on your calendar for a few months down the road? If you've already set a date, keep busting your ass to make it attainable. If you haven't yet and your current career isn't serving you, what are you waiting for? Choose a date six to twelve months down the road and do whatever it takes to make a change so you can build a career that brings you lasting joy.

Chapter 22

The Laws of Attraction & Action

"Whether you think you can, or you think you can't, you're right." - Unknown

The biggest thing holding you back from achieving your dreams and creating a happy life isn't time, money, or opportunity. It's your mind-set.

I want to introduce you to two concepts you may or may not be familiar with: The Law of Attraction and the Law of Action. The Law of Attraction states that our thoughts create our reality. We attract positive or negative experiences into our lives by thinking positive or negative thoughts on a regular basis. It seems like a far-out concept to those who aren't familiar with it, but I promise you, it's not. Some of the most successful people you know have leveraged the Laws of Attraction and Action in their lives, such as Beyoncé, Lady Gaga, Jim Carrey, Oprah Winfrey, Will Smith, Mark Zuckerberg, and Steve Jobs.[41] Leveraging these laws is a competitive advantage for any employee, entrepreneur, or business owner. The Law of Attraction puts you in the mind-set to leverage the Law of Action, or the Law of Cause and Effect. This states that we must engage in actions that support our dreams to make them come true.

There are spiritual elements to the Law of Attraction. Maybe you believe them, maybe you don't. When I first began exploring the Law of Attraction, to be blunt, I thought it was New-Age BS. I thought of the wild-haired people I'd seen at the annual psychic fair my mom attended, with their crystals and palm readings and weirdly restrictive diets.

Turns out, I was being judgmental, and my closed-mindedness prevented me from leveraging one of the most successful business tools and life hacks I've ever come across. Now, I'm not saying you have to believe in the spiritual aspects of the Law of Attraction for it to work in your life, but I ask that you consider it with an open mind.

There is a widely held belief that thoughts emit a kind of energy into the universe. A study in the academic journal *Cosmos and History: The Journal of Natural and Social Philosophy* looked at the measurable impact of Qi, which is an East Asian conception of thought or intentional energy. Researchers found that "Qi has pressure, certain soundwave decibels, changes in heat or infrared, light frequencies, magnetic qualities, and changes [to] chemical reactions, DNA synthesis, cancer cells, and effect on disease and repair of tissue. So we now have characteristics of Qi emission. It is a **fact** [emphasis theirs] that Qi exists and can be."[42] Similarly, a study performed at the University of Arizona studied the "biofield," a conceptual energy field that surrounds all humans and can be theoretically expanded via thought or intention to be perceptible by others. They stated, "The present findings provide compelling basic science support for the hypothesis that humans have varying capacities for biofield awareness and that this capacity is associated with meaningful individual differences."[43] So while not every subject in the study claimed to be able to sense the biofield, a large number were able to have this kind of experience.

Simply put, human beings are magnets. Like attracts like. The Law of Attraction states that the thoughts we send off into the universe will manifest as things and experiences in our lives. So if you focus on doom and gloom, your life will be filled with doom and gloom. If you focus positively on your dreams and goals, you will find a way to accomplish them with massive action.

Noticed I used the words *massive action*. I'm not saying everything you think about will come true. To become a self-made millionaire, you must leverage both the Law of Attraction and the

Law of Action. Ignore either, and chances are, you'll find yourself spinning your wheels.

Research shows that we are attracted to people with positive, joyful attitudes. Baumeister and Leary proposed a fundamental human motivation to form and maintain interpersonal relationships: the "need to belong." Integral to this motivation are signals we instinctively react to, to decide whether to continue or dissolve relationships: Positive affect (e.g., happiness, excitement, enthusiasm) is hypothesized to be linked with creating and maintaining relationships, while negative affect (e.g., anxiety, anger, guilt) is hypothesized to be linked to breaking up relationships."[44] Therefore, if you make positivity a habit, you will have more friends and professional connections, which can be huge for boosting your career. Optimism also makes people want to help you more, further propelling the Law of Attraction to work in your life.

The Power of Visualization

I ignored this powerful mental tool for years because I thought it was too "New Age." It turns out that I haven't found anything that inspires me quite like visualizing does. Have you ever had a conversation with someone about how you would spend your money if you won the lottery? I've had quite a few of these conversations over the years and I always step away feeling *so* excited and ready to make money. (Of course, for most people, this results in buying a lottery ticket, losing, and then letting the excitement fade.)

Pull out your phone or a sheet of paper and do this exercise now. Write down ten things you would do or buy if you won 100 million dollars.

Now pick the most exciting thing on that list and visualize it happening to you, in very specific detail. Maybe it's strolling into a Bugatti dealership and paying cash for a Chiron Sport. Can you *imagine* the look on the salesperson's face? Can you imagine that rush of adrenaline you'd feel driving it off the lot? What would it feel like to walk into your garage and see it sitting there? How would it feel to drive it around town and pick up your best friend for the first time?

Maybe you would pay off your parents' debt. Can you imagine the look on their faces? The tears streaming down their cheeks as they cry and hug you and thank you? *How amazing would that be?*

Or maybe you purchase a mansion on a mountainside or a vacation home in the tropics. What does it look like? If you are having trouble visualizing something, picture motion in your mind: Your dog or cat walking across the marble floors. You sliding down a waterslide in your humongous pool out back. An American flag blowing in the wind by your ten-bedroom beach mansion.

How do you feel right now? Excited? Wishful? I notice that when I do this, it puts me in a completely different state of mind. It gets me excited and ready to manifest the things I've been visualizing!

Now, the problem with this scenario is the chances of winning the lottery are laughably low. One in 175 million. I just did the math, and one in 175 million is roughly 0.000000005714286.

Let's go ahead and round that to 0 percent.

So the lottery isn't our ticket to becoming a millionaire. According to *Business Insider*, your chances of becoming a millionaire if you are under forty years old is one in fifty-five. One in fifty-five is roughly 0.018181818181818.[45]

So we can round that to 2 percent. A little more reasonable, isn't it? You just have to work harder and smarter than fifty-four other people. The fact that you're reading this book proves your success mind-set is in the top 2 percent. I'd bet you could name fifty-four people in your life who aren't reading any self-improvement books.

Now, you may be thinking, *Are the top 2 percent just getting lucky?* Sometimes. Some people luck into wealth or inherit it with little to no effort. But bosses don't rely on luck to make them rich. Chances are, the universe isn't going to hand you a million dollars on a silver platter, no matter how positive your thoughts are. You must be prepared to create your own luck and leverage the Law of Action. As the Roman philosopher Seneca the Younger said, "Luck is what happens when preparation meets opportunity."

Visualization has been a driving force in my motivation for writing this book. Each morning, when I wake up, I imagine myself pouring words onto the page effortlessly, finishing the last sentence, landing a prominent literary agent, flying to New York and meeting with my publishers to seal the deal, then watching my book climb the best seller list. I imagine sipping a glass of champagne with my husband to celebrate being a *New York Times* Best Selling author, beachside, with our toes in the sand.

A couple of months ago, I would wake up and think, "Crap. I should be writing today, but I have so much to do. And last time I sat down to write, I couldn't think of anything to write about. And even if I do think of what to write about, who am I to be giving life advice to other people?"

Until you train your brain to think positively, most people find it's easier to be negative. That's human nature. At our core, we have survival instincts that encourage us to identify threats and always consider the worst possible scenario. It does great things if you're trying to avoid getting eaten by a lion, but it doesn't do anything for your bank account or happiness.

If you practice positivity, you will find motivation. If you find motivation, you'll take action. And if you take action, you will get results and money in the bank. I stay in a positive mind-set by regularly visualizing, meditating, exercising, reading books, and listening to podcasts. I wake up early so I can work on myself before I start working on my business. My morning routine makes me more motivated, productive, and effective throughout the day.

Think You Don't Visualize? Think Again.

We all visualize when we worry. Worrying is simply negative visualization; you're imagining bad or stressful things that could happen and how much those things are going to suck. Think about it! We do it all the time.

Maybe you spend the drive to work worrying about an upcoming project or a headache client. How do you feel after you worry? Anxious. Stressed. Upset. These feelings make us want to curl up in a ball and hide. They prevent action.

Positive visualization has the complete opposite effect. Now, pick one of your biggest dreams and imagine yourself achieving it. Maybe it's starting your own business, writing a book, landing a role in a movie, writing a hit song, being promoted to CEO, or launching a charity to support a cause you really care about.

Now picture the best possible outcome in very specific detail. If you chose starting your own business, for example, you might imagine your business explodes, so you hire a fantastic team and run it remotely as you travel the world. You imagine yourself sitting on the beach being served a savory breakfast, sipping a mimosa, feeling the warm, salty breeze in your hair. Your team is handling your clients, so your day consists of answering a few emails, checking in with key employees, then, perhaps a round of golf or a beach-side massage. Before dinner, you receive the news that you've landed a new client, a six-figure boost to your income. You order whatever you want without even glancing at the prices.

How do you feel now? Excited and inspired?

Worrying kills more dreams than failure ever could. The most successful people realize when they're worrying and do everything in their power to stop themselves. It's not easy and it takes practice, but know that you are in control of your own mind.

The Laws of Attraction and Action don't just work towards money. Here is an example I am experiencing right at this very moment.

I procrastinated writing this book for an entire year because I was letting the Law of Attraction work against me. I was telling myself things like:

- "I have no time to write."

- "I'm already running a successful business. I should just focus on that instead of trying to do too many things at once."

- "I have writer's block," or "I'm not feeling creative today."

- "There are way too many business books out there already. What are the chances mine will be successful?"

- "Who am I to be teaching other people about business? There are plenty of people out there with years more experience than me and much more successful businesses."

I had mentally sold myself on why I *shouldn't* write the book, so I didn't, and for a year, I shoved my dream in my back pocket and went on with my life.

Deep down, I was afraid to fail and I was making excuses. Finally, it dawned on me that I was *already failing*. My business book couldn't possibly be failing more miserably. I didn't even have *one word* written down!

I started telling myself the following things on a daily basis, which inspired me and put me in the right mind-set to actually write this book. I sold myself on why I should write it instead of why I shouldn't:

- "I will make time to write every day, no matter what."

- "I'm running a successful business, which is exactly why I need to write this book! I made over a million dollars at twenty-six years old. I have learned so many lessons that I wish I knew when I graduated college, so I need to get this book out as soon as possible to share that knowledge with others."

- "Creativity is not a finite resource. The more I use, the more I have."

- "I better get my business book out there ASAP before more business books come out. This is the year I will get published and climb the best seller list!

I can tell you with great confidence that you wouldn't be reading this book if I didn't believe and leverage the Laws of Attraction and Action. What could leveraging these laws do for your life?

A Quick Note about Skepticism

Up until this year, I've been a pretty skeptical person. While I'd like to blame it on the crazy world we live in, the more I reflect, I think it's been a personal defense mechanism. I've been slow to trust others and never assumed people's intentions were genuine. Here are some examples:

- A barista at a coffee shop strikes up a conversation with me about my job. She asks me lots of questions and seems interested in my answers. I think, "She's just being nice because it's her job." I'm polite, yet brief in my responses.

- One of my employees compliments a recent website design I've come up with. I say, "Thanks." I think, "She's just sucking up because I'm her manager." I don't dwell on the compliment and quickly move on to another topic.

- One of my favorite authors releases a new motivational training for young entrepreneurs. Instead of being excited, I think, "This training is just a ploy to make money. He doesn't really care about inspiring me. He doesn't even know I exist."

These seem like harmless thoughts, right? I'm sure you can think of a time when you've shrugged off someone's compliment or didn't give someone the benefit of the doubt. A few months ago, it finally dawned on me how harmful these thoughts can be. Let me explain why:

- The barista at the coffee shop just moved into town and doesn't know anyone. She thought I seemed like an interesting person. Because I assumed she was just being nice, I didn't really open up to her. My brevity made me seem standoffish and uninterested in getting to know her. She could've been a great friend or connection down the road, but I'll never know because I assumed she wasn't being genuine.

- The employee genuinely thought my web design was good. She'd studied it over the weekend. She wanted to compliment me on the design and then pick my brain about my creative process, as she is interested in trying website design herself. Because I barely acknowledged her compliment and changed topics of conversation, she thinks, "Maybe my manager isn't interested in teaching me about web design." In reality, I would *love* the help. On top of that, if I truly accepted her compliment was genuine, it would make me feel good, boost my confidence in my design skill-set, and get me even more excited for the next project.

- The author released his training because he is passionate about helping young entrepreneurs. Of course it's an avenue for him to make money, which allows him to live his dream life and continue to inspire others. Had I purchased and listened to the training, I would've felt inspired and ready to kick ass in my business. But because I assumed the author's intentions weren't genuine, I went about my day uninspired.

Realizing this made a monumental difference in my life. I now assume everyone has genuine intentions. (Unless my safety is in question, in which case, I maintain a healthy level of skepticism. I'm not going to hitchhike with a stranger.) But when it comes to people in my daily life, acquaintances, coworkers, friends, and family members, they will always get the benefit of the doubt from me. If they're not being genuine, that's their problem! I now make friends and professional connections easily. My relationships have improved dramatically. And my confidence and motivation levels have reached an all-time high. Why? Because I act much differently now. I will strike up a conversation with anyone and make an effort to connect with them. I accept compliments wholeheartedly and allow them to boost my confidence. I support my favorite authors and inspirational speakers, telling myself, "This book or speech was made to motivate me."

You can and will become rich. You can and will experience a happy life. Believe! Let those positive thoughts take root and grow within you. Visualize your dreams coming to fruition and take massive action to make it happen.

Boss's Action Plan:

1. Write down any negative thoughts you experience.

2. Cross them out and replace them with positive thoughts.

3. Visualize your dreams coming true in great detail. Use this inspiration to motivate yourself to take massive action towards your goals.

4. Keep tabs on your thoughts. If you are being negative, skeptical, or worrying, stop yourself immediately, flip the switch, and think positive thoughts. It may be difficult at first but will become easier and easier with time.

Chapter 23

Health

Earning seven figures is *worthless* if you're too sick or tired to enjoy it. Too often, workaholics are praised for prioritizing wealth over health and mistakenly think you have to sacrifice one for the other. Prioritizing health is a boss's strategy to create energy, which allows you to tackle your dreams and enjoy your wealth while living life to the fullest.

In our society, being healthy is extremely difficult. So many of us sit plopped behind a computer all day, snacking on processed junk and wondering why we're so tired all the time. Health fads come and go. We read an article about the miracle of quinoa and stumble across another article a week later titled, "The Hidden Dangers of Eating Quinoa." There is a lot of confusion around what is healthy and what isn't, which is enough to make many people say, "Why bother? Everything's bad for you. I'm just going to eat whatever I want." In this chapter, we'll get clear about health and why it's important to anyone who wants to make a million dollars and create a happy life.

What Health Is NOT

Health is not judgmental. I've seen so many people who go on diets or health kicks, feeling so motivated and excited in the beginning, but once they give into temptation once or twice for a greasy pizza or rich slice of cake, they completely lose steam. They feel like failures. They beat themselves up. Many times, they'll give up completely and allow themselves to eat, drink, or do whatever they want. I know because I've been there. I've thought, "What's the point? I tried to be healthy and I failed."

Then, I'll plop down on the couch with a bag of potato chips because it seems strangely logical to me.

As we said before, what you focus on expands and becomes your reality. So don't think of health as this horrible thing that forces you to choke down kale and sweat your ass off on a treadmill. A negative perspective of health is one of the biggest reasons why many people struggle with their weight, diet, and efforts to maintain an active lifestyle.

Health is simply the act of caring for your body and mind. Your job is to discover what makes health enjoyable for you.

So you don't like treadmills and gyms? That's fine! Take your dog for a walk. Play tennis or basketball. Sign up for a volleyball league. Garden. Go for a bike ride. Ding-dong ditch your neighbors. Parkour between your coworkers' desks—life is your playground.

Jokes aside, I went through about six months where I barely moved. I walked to the car, drove to work, walked fifty steps to my desk, fifty steps back at the end of the day, then hit the drive-thru and plopped on the couch to watch TV. My energy levels hit rock bottom; I was constantly tired. I kept saying to myself, "Just go outside and take a fifteen-minute walk." But I could never convince myself to actually do it.

Then, one day, while watching a YouTube video on my phone and waiting for my dinner to cook, I started walking around the island in my kitchen, just pacing around in a circle. I watched video after video, and before I knew it, half an hour had passed.

Obviously, kitchen pacing won't turn you into an all-star athlete, but it's a hell of a lot better than just consigning yourself to sitting around all day. To this day, I still pace around my house while listening to TED talks or jotting down ideas for this book. It's something I can commit to and enjoy doing that gets my blood pumping. Physical health doesn't have to be an all-or-nothing approach. Anything more than what you are currently doing is an improvement, so start small and you will be amazed at the strides you can make.

Take on the Mind-Set of More

Health is about adding more: more fruits, vegetables, and nuts, more water, more exercise, more sleep, more time to relax and recharge. Don't focus on the things you can't have. What you focus on consumes your mind and becomes your reality. If you are always thinking about what you can't have, you'll feel constantly deprived, and a feeling of deprivation is why most diets fail.

Personally, I believe a whole-foods, plant-based diet is the healthiest thing you can do for your body. Since going vegan in 2017 and cutting out all animal-based foods from my diet, I've seen a tremendous change in my health and energy levels. When I made this dietary change, I focused on adding more fruits, vegetables, and nuts into my meals, as well as adding more spices and flavorings to create savory dishes that satisfied my cravings without meat or dairy. I always made it about what I could add or try, never about what I couldn't have, and that made all the difference between a diet I dreaded participating in, and one that brought me joy.

Change Your Environment

Don't keep unhealthy food around the house. If healthy is the only option, you take willpower out of the equation. Remember, your job is to find what makes healthy eating enjoyable for you. You may have to experiment with a variety of foods, recipes, restaurants, and grocery stores before you find meals that are both nutritious and delicious.

Create Habits and Sell Yourself on Them

In my experience, habits aren't about constantly resisting temptation; habits are about selling yourself on why those things aren't tempting in the first place. People ask me how I maintain a vegan diet. "How do you have so much willpower? I could never give up steak and cheese. I don't know how you do it."

My secret is that willpower is not even in the equation anymore since I sold myself 100 percent on being vegan. I constantly remind myself of how great I feel when I eat vegan, how confident I feel with my body, how much my blood pressure has improved. I focus on how much I've accomplished with my business and personal brand thanks to my newfound energy levels. What amazing things could you achieve if you sell yourself on developing habits? After all, if you can't sell yourself, how do you expect to sell a customer your product or service?

You are a product of the little decisions you make each day. Habits take the guesswork and willpower out of the equation.

Morning Routines

To most college grads, waking up earlier than you have to seems silly, but once you develop a morning routine of inspiration and self-love, rolling out of bed to go straight to work for someone else will seem ludicrous.

There's a great quote that says, "The brain is a wonderful organ; it starts working the moment you get up in the morning and does not stop until you get into the office." While this may sound funny and relatable to you, life actually doesn't have to be that way.

I've always loved the snooze button and sleeping in, until I experienced the power of a morning routine. A morning routine is time you gift to yourself to improve your physical, mental, and spiritual health. Decide before you go to bed that you're going to wake up thirty to sixty minutes early. When the alarm goes off, don't hit snooze. Smile as you get out of bed, stretch, and brush your teeth. Take the time to make a healthy breakfast, take your vitamins, and get some greens in. (If I don't have time to juice in the morning, I'll drink Perfect Food Raw Organic Green Super-food Powder. You can find this online or at any Whole Foods.) Jot down a few things you're thankful for in a gratitude journal. Watch inspiring YouTube videos, read a self-improvement book, or listen to your favorite podcast. Meditate with an empowering mantra. Get some fresh air and exercise by walking or running outside. Do ten to fifteen minutes of yoga while either repeating an empowering mantra in your head or visualizing yourself smashing through your priority list, small success after small success, each one bringing you closer to your goals. Visualize what it's going to feel like to achieve your dreams, and experience those feelings as deeply as you can. Get yourself excited!

Before my morning routine, I would set my alarm for the latest possible time I could get away with, then rush through my personal hygiene ritual while thinking about how much I wanted to crawl back in bed. Since I was on a time crunch, my day almost always started out on a stressful note. What a monumental difference it makes to spend your morning feeling peaceful, grateful, and inspired, instead of feeling stressed and dreading the day ahead of you.

Taking Breaks & Prioritizing "Me" Time

We've talked about the importance of taking massive action, but no human can live in a constant state of action. Trust me, I've tried on many occasions, and despite my best efforts, I always end up out of steam.

Give yourself permission to take breaks—complete breaks—and set them in your schedule *in stone*. In the next two weeks, I want you to make time for a "Treat Yourself" day (or if you've seen *Parks and Recreation*, "Treat Yo' Self"). It can be a full day or a half day. I do mine once per month, usually on a weekend, but occasionally I'll take off in the middle of the week. Block off your calendar, turn off all notifications, and just do your favorite things!

Maybe it's sleeping in, a round of golf, taking a nap, shopping, hair, nails, video games. Maybe it's refusing to wear pants and binge-watching your favorite TV show. It can be active or lazy. It can be cheap or expensive. It's your day. Treat yo' self.

Taking breaks isn't lazy. Making personal time a priority refuels you to kick ass when you get back to work.

Physical Health Is Just the Tip of the Iceberg

There are so many other areas of health that we must prioritize to experience true wellness. These include mental health, financial health, sexual health, spiritual health, creative health, occupational health, and environmental health. If you neglect yourself in one or more of these areas, fulfillment will elude you. This week, I challenge you to choose one area of health that has gotten the least attention lately and vow to give it the attention it deserves. This could be anything from adopting a new habit to making a huge lifestyle change.

- Maybe your bedroom is constantly messy. You may not realize it, but living in disarray subconsciously causes stress and anxiety. It's hard to feel like you have your life together when the space around you isn't even put together. Commit to one big purging and cleaning session, then vow to put everything away as soon as you're finished using it and leave nothing on the floor. I highly recommend you read *The Life-Changing Magic of Tidying Up* by Marie Kondo, or look up YouTube videos on "KonMari" tidying.

- Maybe your inner child hasn't gotten to play in a while. When you were growing up, your creative outlets were drawing and theater, so sign up to take an art class or join the local community theater—or both!

- Maybe your manager is a jerk who constantly stresses you out. Promise yourself you'll submit one new job application every day this week and that you'll quit this time next month.

At the end of the day, you are the asset, not your business. Your mental, physical, and emotional health is your biggest asset. Prioritizing health is a strategic business move that sets you apart from your unhealthy, overworked competitors. What health habit can you start today that your future self will thank you for?

Your Dream Life
Is Yours To Create

By now, you know what it takes to be a boss and exactly how I became a twenty-seven-year-old millionaire.

**Ready to earn seven figures
and build your dream life?**

The first step is to convince yourself you can and *will* achieve your wildest dreams. You owe it to yourself to work towards your goals today, not tomorrow, not next week or next year. Make a decision, believe it will happen, and develop a daily habit that propels you forward. Block out time for this habit in your schedule every day, no matter what. Commit to improving yourself, your health, and your happiness consistently, learning to ignore the negative and focus on the positive, because what you focus on expands. Learn what ignites your inner spark so you can get yourself in the zone on a daily basis.

It's only after you've harnessed this inner power that you can attract success into your life, earn seven figures, and make an impact on the world. Customers, mentors, friends, and other bosses flock to those who are genuine, confident, hardworking, and happy—those who add value to the lives of others. Know that I am describing *you*. Every day, these words will describe you more and more as you develop good habits and build your emotional muscle.

You've learned how to eliminate debt, create financial abundance, land a job at a fast-growing company, free your time, and launch and scale a business on your terms. Most importantly, you know how and why you should prioritize your health and happiness.

**You can have absolutely *anything*
you want in this world.**

Go forth and kick ass, my fellow boss. The world has magnificent things in store for you. You deserve all the happiness and success this life has to offer. The power lies within you.

For more resources, visit www.whycollegeisbroken.com. To elevate your network and develop a powerful circle of influence, visit www.bossesandbreadwinners.com.

Thank you for reading College is Broken: How To Create A Life of Wealth & Freedom While Most Graduates Are Broke, Stressed, & Moving Back In With Their Parents. If this book impacted you in some way, do me a favor and buy a copy for a friend. This world needs more bosses like you.

Acknowledgments

I'd like to thank my father and Papaw for giving me the entrepreneurial bug.

My mother for teaching me how to talk to anyone and do anything I set my mind to, and for introducing me to the world of energy and meditation.

My incredible editors Elizabeth, Becky, and mom for nitpicking my rough draft into a book.

My husband for being my biggest supporter and for reading this book despite the fact that he hates reading.

My amazing team at Creekmore Marketing, who worked so hard to take day-to-day responsibilities off my plate so I could bring this book into the world. Shoutout to Emma Brown for designing the cover of this book!

My mentors Peter Voogd and Mark Lack for helping me position this book and take my dreams to the next level.

The founding chapter of Bosses & Breadwinners for sparking me in remarkable ways and showing me how powerful a circle of influence can be.

And all the friends and family members who supported me, got excited with me, and believed in me since the beginning.

Recommended Resources

Recommended Reading

- *The Power of Habit* by Charles Duhigg

- *The Compound Effect* by Darren Hardy

- *6 Months to 6 Figures* and *The Entrepreneur's Blueprint to Massive Success* by Peter Voogd

- *The One Thing* by Gary W. Keller and Jay Papasan

- *Procrastinate on Purpose* by Rory Vanden

- *The Total Money Makeover* by Dave Ramsey

- *How to Win Friends & Influence People* by Dale Carnegie

- *The Difference Maker: Making Your Attitude Your Greatest Asset* by John C. Maxwell

- *The Ten Times Rule* by Grant Cardone

- *The Life-Changing Magic of Tidying Up* by Marie Kondo

Recommended Viewing

- Rory Vaden's TED talk on "How to Multiply Your Time"

- Gen Kelsang Nyema's TED talk "Happiness Is All in Your Mind"

Recommended Podcasts

- Please Finish Your Book! by Shola Richards

- The War of Art: Breaking Through the Blocks and Win Your Inner Creative Battles by Steven Pressfield

Recommended Apps

- Calm

- Headspace

Resources

- SendOutCards: www.creekmorecards.com

- CVI Assessment: members.taylorprotocols.com/Tools/CVIGift.aspx?GiftHash=a6d9f914-5adb-1030-aa1a-adf0ab89abbd

- Places to Sell Stock Photography: https://www.shawacademy.com/blog/10-places-sell-stock-photography/

Develop An Abundance Mindset

- Here is a powerful free guide of 100 Money Affirmations I Used To Make 6-Figures (In Less Than 6 Months). You can download the affirmations in both print and audio formats, as well as access free wall prints and beautiful phone backgrounds with your favorite affirmations on them at: https://www.whycollegeisbroken.com/money.

Find Freelancers

- Upwork.com

- 99designs.com

- Fiverr.com

Mastering Sales Resources

- https://www.omnicalculator.com/business/margin

Become an Influencer

- https://www.dictionary.com/browse/influencer

Master Your Time

- http://www.apa.org/research/action/multitask.aspx

Find Likeminded Entrepreneurs

- http://www.bossesandbreadwinners.com

Reminders:

I've created a list of automation tools and platforms you can find in the Resources section of this book or online at www.whycollegeisbroken.com.

About Chelsea Creekmore

Chelsea Creekmore is a self-made millionaire and serial entrepreneur. She graduated college in a mountain of debt with no clue how to manage finances—with a business degree but no clue how to actually start a business. She felt cheated. Wasn't her degree supposed to be her ticket to success and stability?

She started Creekmore Marketing at the ripe age of twenty-two, in bed, in her PJs, with big dreams and little experience. She went from broke to seven figures in four years by going all in after her dreams and unsubscribing from the play-it-safe advice she'd been given her entire life. Today, Creekmore Marketing is a multimillion-dollar company with a staff of forty and clients all over the country.

Chelsea despises society's norms: how we encourage young minds to plug and chug their way through the education system for a piece of paper, climb their way up the corporate ladder even if it means missing their kids' soccer games, and then retire when they're too old and sick to enjoy the fruits of their labor. She discovered a different path that led to more freedom, fulfillment, and financial abundance than she ever imagined. Her mission is to inspire people around the world to do the same.

She is the founder of Bosses & Breadwinners, a mastermind group for entrepreneurs who want to take their lives and businesses to the next level. Each chapter meets regularly to brainstorm, mastermind, support, and inspire each other. If you have big dreams and haven't found your tribe yet, apply to join or start a chapter in your city at www.bossesandbreadwinners.com.

Notes

1 "The NCES Fast Facts Tool Provides Quick Answers to Many Education Questions (National Center for Education Statistics)." National Center for Education Statistics (NCES) Home Page, a part of the U.S. Department of Education, 2017. https://nces.ed.gov/fastfacts/display.asp?id=76.

2 Clifton, Jim. "The World's Broken Workplace." Gallup.com. Gallup, December 9, 2019. https://news.gallup.com/opinion/chairman/212045/world-broken-workplace.aspx.

3 Federal Reserve Bank of New York, The Labor Market for Recent College Graduates, Underemployment https://www.newyorkfed.org/research/college-labor-market/index.html

4 Burning Glass Technologies and Strada Institute for the Future of Work (2018) , "The Permanent Detour: Underemployment's Long-Term Effects on the Careers of College Grads"

5 U.S. Department of Education. Institute of Education Sciences, National Center for Education Statistics (2018). Digest of Education Statistics, Table 502.10, Supporting Crosswalk SOC Table, https://nces.ed.gov/ipeds/resource/download/IPEDS_HR_2018_SOC_Crosswalk.pdf

6 U.S. Department of Education. Institute of Education Sciences, National Center for Education Statistics (2018). Digest of Education Statistics, Table 330.10

7 U.S. Census Bureau, Real Median Household Income in the United States [MEHOINUSA672N], retrieved from FRED, Federal Reserve Bank of St. Louis; https://fred.stlouisfed.org/series/MEHOINUSA672N, December 8, 2019

8 Official Cohort Default Rates for Schools. (n.d.). Retrieved December 8, 2019, from https://www2.ed.gov/offices/OSFAP/defaultmanagement/cdr.html.

9 Bialik, K., & Fry, R. (2019, February 14). How Millennials compare with prior generations. Retrieved from https://www.pewsocialtrends.org/essay/millennial-life-how-young-adulthood-today-compares-with-prior-generations/.

10 Student Debt Removes Embarrassment for Young Americans Moving Back Home... For Years. (2019, June 6). Retrieved from https://www.amtd.com/news-and-stories/press-releases/press-release-details/2019/Student-Debt-Removes-Embarrassment-for-Young-Americans-Moving-Back-Home-For-Years/default.aspx.

11 James Clear, "How Long Does It Actually Take to Form a New Habit? (Backed by Science)," https://jamesclear.com/new-habit. The myth that it takes twenty-one days to thirty days to form a habit actually comes from a plastic surgeon who worked in the 1950s named Dr. Maxwell Maltz. Maltz noticed that his patients who came in for facial augmentation reported a delay of around twenty-one days to get used to their new facial features. He published this observation in a book titled Psycho-Cybernetics that was released in 1960 and went on to be a best seller. It is generally believed that this adage came from people taking Maltz's observation out of context.

12 Phillippa Lally, Cornelia H. M. van Jaarsveld, Henry W. W. Potts, and Jane Wardle, "How Are Habits Formed: Modelling Habit Formation in the Real World," European Journal of Social Psychology 40 (6) (10)(2010), 1002, http://libdata.lib.ua.edu/login?url=https://search.ebscohost.com/login.aspx?direct=true&db=aph&AN=53843531&site=eds-live&scope=site.

13 Anthony Cilluffo, "5 Facts about Student Loans," Fact Tank, August 24, 2017.

14 Cilluffo, 2017.

15 Erin Dunlop Velez, Jennie H. Woo, National Center for Education Statistics and RTI International, "The Debt Burden of Bachelor's Degree Recipients. Stats in Brief," National Center for Education Statistics 1 (2017), http://libdata.lib.ua.edu/login?url=https://search.ebscohost.com/login.aspx?direct=true&db=eric&AN=ED573698&site=eds-live&scope=site.

16 Josh Mitchell, "Mike Meru Has $1 Million in Student Loans. How Did That Happen? Escalating Tuition and Easy Credit Have Yielded a Class of Student-Loan Borrowers with Spectacular Debt They May Never Pay Back," Wall Street Journal, May 25, 2018.

17 Federal Student Aid Repayment Estimator in US Department of Education, accessed November 6, 2018, https://studentloans.gov/myDirectLoan/mobile/repayment/repaymentEstimator.action#view-repayment-plans.

18 David Garland, "Seth Godin on the Big Differences between an Entrepreneur and a Freelancer," 2011 in Rise to the Top, podcast.

19 Susan Roane, "The Secrets of Savvy Networking," accessed December 5, 2018, https://www.susanroane.com/the-secrets-of-savvy-networking/.

20 Rackham, Neil. Spin Selling. New York: McGraw Hill Book Company, 1988.

21 John Ternieden, "Grant Cardone's 7 Simple Tips to Improve Sales Follow-Up," Inside Sales (2016).

22 Carl Buehner, Richard Evans' Quote Book (Publisher's Press, 1971).

23 "Understanding the Pareto Principle (the 80/20 Rule)," BetterExplained, accessed December 6, 2018, https://betterexplained.com/articles/understanding-the-pareto-principle-the-8020-rule/.

24 Walter Isaacson, "The Real Leadership Lessons of Steve Jobs," Harvard Business Review (Spring 2012).

25 Keller, Gary, and Jay Papasan. The One Thing: The Surprisingly Simple Truth behind Extraordinary Results. Austin, TX: Bard Press, 2017.

26 Vaden, Rory. "How to Multiply Your Time." Speech, TEDxDouglasville, Douglasville, GA, July 14, 2019. https://www.youtube.com/watch?v=y2X7c9TUQJ8

27 Isaacson, Walter. "The Real Leadership of Steve Jobs." Harvard Business Review, April 2012. Accessed July 14, 2019. https://hbr.org/2012/04/the-real-leadership-lessons-of-steve-jobs.

28 Stephen Covey, "Restoring the Character Ethic," in The Seven Habits of Highly Effective People (New York: RosettaBooks LLC, 1989), 161.

29 David Evans MacDonnell, 1798. "Dictionary of Quotations in Most Frequent Use," The Monthly Review. 467.

30 Mark, Gloria, Daniela Gudith, and Ulrich Klocke. "The Cost of Interrupted Work: More Work and More Stress." Proceedings of the SIGCHI Conference on Human Factors in Computing Systems, 2008, 107-10. Accessed July 15, 2019. https://www.ics.uci.edu/~gmark/chi08-mark.pdf.

31 Steve Nguyen, "Multitasking Doesn't Work," Workplace Psychology (April 4, 2011), https://workplacepsychology.net/2011/04/04/multitasking-doesnt-work/.

32 Jose Vasquez, "How Much Time Do You Waste in Meetings?" The Huffington Post (May 30, 2017), https://www.huffingtonpost.com/entry/how-much-time-do-you-waste-in-meetings_us_592d7c23e4b08861ed0ccbf2.

33 Rory Vaden, "Money Value of Time," The Huffington Post (December 7, 2017), https://www.huffpost.com/entry/money-value-of-time_n_4453136.

34 Scott, Kim Malone. Radical Candor: Be a Kick-ass Boss without Losing Your Humanity. S.l.: St Martins Press, 2019.

35 Nyema, Gen Kelsang. "Happiness Is All in Your Mind." Lecture, TEDxGreenville, Greenville, SC, July 23, 2019. https://www.youtube.com/watch?v=xnLoToJVQH4

36 Mark Twain, Mark Twain's Notebook, ed. Albert Bigelow Paine (1935) 393.

37 Robert T. Kiyosaki. Rich Dad, Poor Dad: What the Rich Teach Their Kids About Money That the Poor and Middle Class Do Not! New York City, NY: Warner Books, Inc., 1998.

38 Lindsay Jacobs and Suphanit Piyapromdee. 2016. Labor Force Transitions at Older Ages: Burnout, Recovery, and Reverse Retirement. Washington, D.C.: Federal Reserve Board, 053. 1.

39 Shan P. Tsai, Judy K. Wendt, Robin P. Donnelly, Geert De Jong, and Farah S. Ahmed. 2005. "Age at Retirement and Long Term Survival of an Industrial Population: Prospective Cohort Study," BMJ 331 (7523) (October 29).

40 "Want to Live a Long Life? Don't Retire Early," The Health Site, 2016, accessed December 10, 2018, https://www.thehealthsite.com/news/want-to-live-a-long-life-dont-retire-early-ag0416/.

41 "15 Stars Who Use the Law of Attraction, The Talko, https://www.the-talko.com/15-stars-who-use-the-law-of-attraction/.

42 Phillip Shinnick and Laurence Porter, "Difficulties in Inorganic and Organic Measurement of Energy: Influences of Mind (Intention or Yi) and Nature in Outcome," Cosmos and History: The Journal of Natural and Social Philosophy 1 (2018), 187, http://libdata.lib.ua.edu/login?url=https://search.ebscohost.com/login.aspx?direct=true&db=edsglr&AN=edsgcl.533004795&site=eds-live&scope=site.

43 L. A. Nelson and G. E. Schwartz, "Human Biofield and Intention Detection: Individual Differences," Journal of Alternative & Complementary Medicine

11 (2005) Issue 1, Vol. 2. 93–101, http://lib-data.lib.ua.edu/login?url=https://search.ebscohost.com/login.aspx?direct=true&db=rzh&AN=106612400&site=eds-live&scope=site. 98.

44 Jeffrey R. Vittengl and Craig S. Holt, "Getting Acquainted: The Relationship of Self-Disclosure and Social Attraction to Positive Affect," Journal of Social & Personal Relationships 17 (1) (Feb. 2000), 54.

45 Ana Swanson. "Your Chance of Becoming a Millionaire Depends a Lot on Your Age." Business Insider. Business Insider, August 4, 2015. https://www.businessinsider.com/your-chance-of-becoming-a-millionaire-depends-a-lot-on-your-age-2015-8.

www.ingramcontent.com/pod-product-compliance
Lightning Source LLC
Chambersburg PA
CBHW060045100426
42742CB00014B/2702